AF316734

This book is dedicated
to my teachers,
parents and all the
students

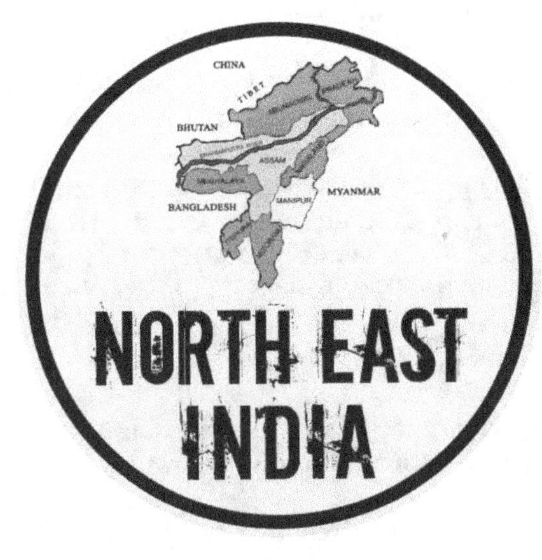

About the Author

Rajat Paul is an educator, Blogger, and knowledge-based content creator.

Junior Assistant at Assam Financial Corporation, Government of Assam.

Cashier (Gr-II) at Assam State Warehousing Corporation, Government of Assam.

Education: B.COM (Hons) from Gauhati Commerce College, M.COM (Hons) from Calcutta University, PGDHRM from Tezpur University, DFA from NIIT, Master in Travel and Tourism Management, Certified Financial Planner (CFP) (Final).

Educator: 5+ years of teaching experience in YouTube for competitive exams.

Awards: 1. Best content writer of 2020's Assam Tourism Development Corporation competition. 2. Assam Book of Record winner.

Administrator of Facebook Page: Northeast India (Sharing of Daily News and Important General Knowledge).

I wish everyone all the very best and suggestions are welcomed at my e-mail I'd which is rajatpaul304@gmail.com.

Follow My YouTube Channel: Northeast India for more updates.

Contents:

HISTORY OF BANKING AND FINANCE IN ANCIENT INDIA

1. The Vedic word Kusidin refers to.
Ans: Usurer (A person who lends money at a high rate of interest)

2. The loan deeds in the Vedic period are called
Ans: Rnapatra or Rnalekha

3. Who wrote Arthashastra?
Ans: Kautilya

4. The Arthashastra of Kautilya mentions the presence of Bankers in which era?
Ans: Maurya

5. Name the instruments in the Maurya era which are equivalent to the bill of exchange in recent times.
Ans: Adesha

6. Manusmriti was written by
Ans: Manu (laws of Manu or Manava Dharmashastra)

7. The businessmen called by names of Shroffs, Seths, Sahukars, Mahajans, Chettis, etc. had been carrying on the business of _____ since ancient times.
Ans: Banking

HISTORY OF BANKING:

We will discuss the history of banking in 3 phases.
Phase I: Pre-Independence 1770 to 1947
Phase II: Post-Independence 1947-1991 (The Nationalization Phase 1969 to 1991)
Phase III: Liberalization or Banking Sector Reforms Phase 1991 to present.

Phase I: The Pre-Independence Phase

1. Name the first bank of India.
Ans: "Bank of Hindustan", established in 1770, located in Calcutta (capital of India during that time). Stopped operations in 1832.

2. The General Bank of India was established in which year, by whom, and where?
Ans: 1786, East India Company, Calcutta. (the second oldest bank in India)

3. Name the country's first commercial bank?
Ans: Oudh Commercial Bank was established in the year 1881 and stopped working in 1958.

4. The Bank of Bengal was established in the year?
Ans: 2 January 1809, (Initially it was Bank of Calcutta, established on 2 June 1806)

5. The Bank of Bombay was established in the year?
Ans: 1840

6. The Bank of Madras was established in the year?
Ans: 1843

7. Who established the three banks, Bank of Bengal, Bank of Bombay, and Bank of Madras?
Ans: The East India Company or British.

8. The Bank of Bengal, Bank of Bombay, and Bank of Madras, known as?
Ans: Presidential Banks.

9. At which place, did the East India Company establish its first presidency bank?
Ans: Calcutta

10. The Bank of Bengal, Bank of Bombay, and Bank of Madras were later merged into one single bank in 1921, called?
Ans: The "Imperial Bank of India."
(The Imperial Bank of India was later nationalized in 1955 and was named The State Bank of India)

11. The founder and headquarter of Imperial Bank of India is?
Ans: John Maynard Keynes, Bombay.

12. Name the oldest public-Sector bank of India?

Ans: Allahabad Bank was established in 1865. Presently Allahabad Bank has been merged with Indian Bank.

13. Which is the oldest Joint Stock bank of India?
Ans: Allahabad Bank
Allahabad Bank was established in 1865
Punjab National Bank was established in 1894
Bank of India was established in 1906
Canara Bank was established in 1906
Bank of Baroda was established in 1908
Central Bank of India was established in 1911

14. Name the first bank of limited liabilities managed by Indians and founded in 1881 was?
Ans: Oudh Commercial Bank

15. Which was the first Bank incorporated by the Indians?
Ans: Avadh Commercial Bank (Oudh Commercial Bank)

16. The first ever wholly Indian Bank was set up in which year and name the Bank?
Ans: In 1894, and Punjab National Bank was set up in Lahore (earlier British India) entirely using Indian capital.

17. The origin of the State Bank of India goes back to the first decade of the 19th century with the establishment of?
Ans: Bank of Calcutta

18. The Largest and Oldest Bank still in existence is
Ans: State Bank of India

Phase II: The Post Independence Period (1947-1991) (Including Nationalization Phase from 1969-1991)

19. Indian government nationalized banks under which Act?
Ans: Banking Regulation Act, 1949

20. How many banks were Nationalized on 19th June 1969, the first nationalization of banks, and what was the benchmark of the national deposits?
Ans: 14 Banks, banks whose national deposits were more than 50 crores.

21. How many banks were Nationalized on the year 15th April 1980, the second phase of nationalization?
Ans: 6 banks

22. When was the SBI formed?
Ans: 1 July 1955, under the SBI Act of 1955. On that day the Imperial Bank of India was renamed SBI.

23. Which bank acquired the majority stake of the SBI when it was formed on 1 July 1955 by transferring its name from the Imperial Bank of India?
Ans: Reserve Bank of India (60%)

24. How many subsidiary banks belong to SBI?
Ans: 7. (State Bank of Patiala, State Bank of Hyderabad, State Bank of Bikaner & Jaipur, State Bank of Mysore, State Bank of Travancore, State Bank of Saurashtra, State Bank of Indore)

25. Name the last subsidiary bank that merged with SBI.
Ans: State Bank of Indore, which merged in 2010.

Phase III: The Liberalization Period (1991-Till Date)

26. India's New Economic Policy or Liberalization Privatization Globalization (LPG) happened in the year?
Ans: 1991

27. To provide stability and profitability to the Nationalized Public sector Banks, the Government decided to set up a committee under the leadership of?
Ans: Shri. M Narasimham.

28. Who managed the various reforms in the Indian banking industry in 1991?
Ans: Shri. M Narasimham

29. In which year and under which policy Private sector banks were introduced in India and the RBI give away licenses to 10 Private sector banks to establish themselves in the country?
Ans: New Economic Policy or Liberalization Privatization Globalization (LPG) of 1991.

30. Under whose government New Economic Policy happened and who was the finance minister then?
Ans: P. V. Narasimha Rao was the Prime Minister and Manmohan Singh was the finance minister.

HISTORY OF BANKING (ASSAM)

1. Reserve Bank of India has set up a Committee on Financial Sector Development in 2006 for the NER under the Chairmanship of?
Ans: Deputy Governor, Ms. Usha Thorat.

2. Name the Northeast India's first small finance bank which was opened in 2018?
Ans: Northeast Small Finance bank (NESFB) previously RGVN microfinance.

3. Which bank has inaugurated the first ever "All Women Branch" in Northeast India in Dec 2016 and where?
Ans: Axis Bank, Uzan bazar Branch, Guwahati, Assam.

4. Name the first ever bank established in the Northeast India?
Ans: The Guwahati Bank Ltd was established on 18th June 1926. It was a non-government company and classified as "company limited by shares.

5. Who established the first ever bank in the Northeast India and where?
Ans: Lt. Gauri Kanta Talukdar, set up in the house of the former at Latasil, Ambari, Guwahati.

6. In which year the Guwahati bank ltd had got its permanent address at the Panbazaar, in the two-storied building opposite the Panbazar Masjid, now housed by the Central Bank of India, Panbazar Branch in Guwahati?
Ans: 1936.

7. Name the first Director and Manager of The Guwahati Bank Ltd?
Ans: The first Director was Lokpriya Gopinath Bordoloi, and the first Manager was Upen Changkakoti.

8. How many branches did the bank had?

Ans: The bank had 12 branches in Assam and also a branch in Kolkata.

9. In which year it was recognised by the Assam Government and subsequently listed with the RBI?
Ans: 1940.

10. In which year it was closed and suspended all its operations?
Ans: On 20th July 1950, the bank suspended operations due to economic downfall.

11. Name the only regional rural bank of Assam, India?
Ans: Assam Gramin Vikash Bank

12. When was Assam Gramin Vikash Bank formally launched?
Ans: 12 January 2006

13. Assam Gramin Vikash Bank was formed on 12 January 2006 after the amalgamation of Pragjyotish Gaonlia Bank, Lakhimi Gaonlia Bank, Cachar Gramin Bank and ____?
Ans: Subansiri Gaonlia Bank.

14. On 1 April 2019 Assam Gramin Vikash Bank was further amalgamated with ____ bank, which is also the last bank on which Assam Gramin Vikash Bank got Amalgamated and finally formed the present-day Assam Gramin Vikash Bank?
Ans: Langpi Dehangi Rural Bank

15. How many tiers structure does the Assam Gramin Vikash Bank have?
Ans: Three tier structure consisting of one head office at Guwahati, nine regional offices and 473 branches.

16. RRBs are owned by how many entities?
Ans: 3 / Three

16. Assam Gramin Vikash Bank is owned by Government of India (50%), Government of Assam (15%) and ____?

Ans: Punjab National Bank (35%)

17. Name the first woman from Assam who founded and runs a Co-operative bank?
Ans: Lakhimi Baruah

18. Name the first woman from Assam who founded and runs the first all-woman Co-operative bank of Assam.
Ans: Lakhimi Baruah

19. Name the first all-woman bank of Assam?
Ans: Konoklata Mahila Urban Cooperative Bank for women. The bank employs only women.

20. Name the bank which was founded by Lakhimi Baruah?
Ans: Konoklata Mahila Urban Cooperative Bank for women

21. When and where was the Konoklota Mahila Urban Cooperative Bank for women established?
Ans: In 1998, Jorhat city.

22. With an initial investment of how many rupees, Lakhimi Baruah set up her Co-operative bank?
Ans: Rs. 8.45 lakh and 1,500 women members.

23. In 2021 Lakhimi Baruah was awarded the ______ by the President of India and Republic of India, for contributions and efforts to financially empower women of Assam.
Ans: Padma Shri, the fourth-highest civilian award.

RESERVE BANK OF INDIA

About Reserve Bank of India

1. When was the Reserve Bank of India established and under which act?
Ans: 1st April 1935 under the RBI act 1934.

2. The Reserve Bank of India works under which laws and rules of the Government of India?
Ans: RBI act 1934.

3. Under the recommendation of which Committee Reserve Bank of India was formed?
Ans: "Royal Commission of Indian Currency and Finance" also called "Hilton Young Committee".

4. When was the Reserve Bank of India Nationalized?
Ans: 1 January 1949.

5. Where was the first headquarters of RBI?
Ans: Calcutta (1935-1937) Now, Mumbai

6. When did the Central Office / Headquarter of the Reserve Bank permanently move to Mumbai?
Ans: In 1937.

7. What is the logo of the Reserve Bank of India?
Ans: Tiger/Panther and Tree (Palm)

8. How many Zonal Offices are there?
Ans: 4, (New Delhi - north, Kolkata - east, Chennai - south, Mumbai - west)

9. How many Regional Offices are there?
Ans: 27 (total 31 offices)

10. How many Sub-Offices are there?
Ans: 04 (total 31 offices)

11. The Reserve Bank's affairs are governed by a central board of directors. Who appoints the board in keeping with the Reserve Bank of India Act.
Ans: Government of India

12. The Board of Directors are appointed /nominated for a period of ____ years.
Ans: four

13. Under the RBI Act 1934, under sec 8(1)(a), RBI has 1 Governor and how many Deputy Governors under the Central Board of Directors?
Ans: 4 (four)

14. Under the RBI Act 1934, how many deputy governors can be appointed at maximum?
Ans: 4 (four)

15. How many Central Board of Directors are there in RBI under the RBI act in 1934?
Ans: fifteen

16. From all the fifteen directors that come under the Central Board of Directors appointed /nominated under RBI Act, 1934, how many are official directors?
Ans: five (one governor and four Dy Governors) (Rest ten are Non-Official Directors)

17. Under the Central Board of Directors appointed /nominated under RBI Act, 1934, how many non-official directors are appointed/nominated from local boards?
Ans: four (Local Boards consist of Western Area, Eastern Area, Northern Area and Southern Area)

18. Name the 1st Governor of RBI?
Ans: Osborne Smith (non-Indian) 1935-37

19. Name the 1st Indian governor of RBI?
Ans: C D Deshmukh in 1937

20. Name the 1st CFO of RBI?
Ans: Sudha Balakrishnan

21. Name the person who has handled the post of RBI Governor And Prime Minister of India?
Ans: Manmohan Singh.

22. Name the person who has handled the post of RBI Governor, Financial Secretary of India and Prime Minister of India?
Ans: Manmohan Singh.

23. What is the Tenure of Governor of the Reserve Bank of India?
Ans: 3 years can be extended up to 5 years.

24. People call the Reserve Bank of India with other names such as-
Ans: Banker's bank, Apex bank, Banker to last resort.

25. Name the first woman to become Deputy governor of RBI?
Ans: K J Udeshi 2008

26. Name the subsidiary organizations of RBI?
Ans: The organizations are:
1. DICGC (Deposit Insurance and Credit Guarantee Corporation)
2. BRBNMPL (Bharatiya Reserve Bank Note Mudran Pvt Ltd)
3. Reserve Bank Information Technology Private Limited (ReBIT),
4. Indian Financial Technology and Allied Services (IFTAS),
5. Reserve Bank Innovation Hub (RBIH)

Deposit Insurance and Credit Guarantee Corporation (DICGC): Formed in 15 July 1978 and headquartered in Mumbai, this premier serves as a specialized division or a subsidiary organization of Reserve Bank of India, Ministry of Finance, Government of India. The organization is governed under the legal provisions of 'The Deposit Insurance and Credit Guarantee Corporation Act, 1961' (DICGC Act).

Primary functions: The primary and the sole function of the former is to insure all bank deposits (such as saving, fixed, current, recurring) for up to the limit of Rs. 500,000 of each depositor in a bank. This means that if the bank fails or gets liquidated the depositors will receive a maximum amount of Rs 5 lakh against their account.

Some points to be noted: 1. A maximum of ₹5,00,000 is insured for each user for both principal and interest amount. 2. If the customer has accounts in different branches of the same bank, all of those accounts are insured to a maximum of ₹5,00,000 each. 3. If there are more accounts in same bank, all of those are treated as a single account. 4. Since it is a insurance against the deposits the insurance premium is paid by the insured banks, this means the insurance protection is made available to the depositors or customers of banks free of cost. 5. The Corporation has the power to cancel the registration of an insured bank if it fails to pay the premium for three consecutive half-year periods.

Note: Past 2017, the insured amount was just Rs 1 lakh, but in 2017, the Government of India introduced the Financial Resolution and Deposit Insurance bill, 2017 in order to bring these reforms.

Bharatiya Reserve Bank Note Mudran Private Ltd (BRBNMPL): Founded on 3 February 1995, headquartered in Bangalore as a wholly owned subsidiary of Reserve Bank of India under the jurisdiction of the Ministry of finance of the Government of India.

Primary function: The organization currently caters the demand of Indian rupee notes from designing, printing and supplying. In a simple sense it mints banknotes.

BRBNMPL has two presses in Mysuru (Karnataka) and Salboni (West Bengal). It has its own design cell with the capability to print all the denominations of Indian bank notes. It made a world record by printing more than 20,000 million pieces of bank notes in the financial year 2016 - 17.

A Learning and Development Centre of the Bharatiya Reserve Bank Note Mudran Private Limited

(BRBNMPL) has been established in Mysuru, Karnataka. LDC is being established with active collaboration from Security Printing and Minting Corporation of India Limited (SPMCIL) and Bank Note Paper Mill India Private Limited (BNPMIPL). LDC will act as a forum for robust knowledge dissemination, thus ensuring that the best practices, experiences, and innovations are shared efficiently in a congenial environment to ensure uniformity in banknote production, quality and supply.

BRBNMPL has a subsidiary agency named Security Printing and Minting Corporation of India Limited (SPMCIL).

Security Printing and Minting Corporation of India Ltd: Founded on 10 February 2006, headquartered in New Delhi, it is a Government Printing and Minting Agency, a subsidiary organization of BRBNMPL under the jurisdiction of the Ministry of Finance, Government of India.

The primary function of the corporation is to manufacture currency and banknotes, security paper, non-judicial stamp papers, postage stamps and stationery, travel document viz., passport and visa, security certificates, cheques, bonds, warrants, special certificates with security features, security inks, circulation and commemorative coins, medallions, refining of gold, silver and assay of precious metals.

Until 1928, Indian currency was printed by De La Rue, a British banknote manufacturing company. The Indian Security Press at Nashik was commissioned by the British Indian Government in the same year and assigned the responsibility of printing Indian currency.

It was established in 2006 after the corporatization of presses and mints (nine units viz four mints, four presses and a paper mill) functioning under the Indian Ministry of Finance. The nine units include two bank note presses viz Currency Note Press at Nashik Maharashtra and Bank Note Presses at Dewas (MP), two security presses at Nashik and Hyderabad, four mints at Mumbai, Kolkata, Hyderabad and Noida and one security paper mill at Hoshangabad.

In Details: SPMCIL broadly operates through four production verticals i.e. currency printing presses, security printing presses, security paper mill and India Government mints.

Currency printing presses: SPMCIL consists of two currency printing presses: the Currency Note Press (CNP) in Nashik and the Bank Note Press (BNP) in Dewas. The two units are engaged in production of bank notes for India as well as a few foreign countries including Iraq, Nepal, Sri Lanka, Myanmar and Bhutan. More than 40% of Currency Notes circulated in India are printed by the two units.

Currency Note Press (CNP) in Nashik was established in 1928 as the first printing press for bank notes in India.

Security printing presses: SPMCIL consist of two Security printing presses namely the India Security Press (ISP) at Nashik and Security Printing Press (SPP) at Hyderabad. These presses print the 100% requirement of passports and other travel documents, non-judicial stamp papers, cheques, bonds, warrants, postal stamps and postal stationery and other security products.

Mints: SPMCIL comprises four units of India Government Mint located in the cities of Mumbai, Kolkata, Hyderabad and Noida. These mints produce circulation coins, commemorative coins, medallions and bullion, as required by the Government of India.

Paper mill: Security Paper Mill was established in 1968 at Hoshangabad, Madhya Pradesh. It produces papers for banknotes and non–judicial stamps and further prints with new enhanced unit.

Reserve Bank Information Technology Private Limited (ReBIT):
Reserve Bank Information Technology Private Limited (ReBIT), has been set up by the Reserve Bank of India to serve its IT and cybersecurity needs and to improve the cyber resilience of the Indian banking industry.

Indian Financial Technology & Allied Services (IFTAS): Established in 2015 by the Institute for Development and Research in Banking Technology (IDRBT), an autonomous organization funded by the Reserve Bank of India, it is a Not-for-profit company, registered under the provisions of Section 8 of Indian Companies Act, 2013.

The primary function is to design, deploy & provide the essential IT-related services that are required by the Reserve Bank of India, banks, and other financial institutions. **Some of its services and products include:**

1. Indian Financial Network (INFINET) is the underlying closed user group Payment System network connecting India's financial institutions.

2. Structured Financial Messaging System (SMS) serves as the backbone Messaging platform and the Indian standard for inter-bank Financial Messaging for Centralized Payment system viz. National Electronic Fund Transfer (NEFT) and Real-Time Gross Settlement (RTGS).

3. Global Interchange for Financial Transactions (GIFT), is an integrated Payment & Settlement system that has been created to provide straight-through processing (SP) inter-bank transactions, supporting batched, gross & bulk settlement modes.

Reserve Bank Innovation Hub (RBIH): Formed in 2022, headquartered in Bengaluru, a section 8 company formed under the Companies Act, 2013, with an initial capital contribution of Rs 100 crore in order to promote and facilitate an environment that accelerates innovation across the financial sector.

The primary objective of this company is to position India as a global innovation hub for a network of financial services providers, fintech innovation hubs, policymakers, technologists, academia, and the investor community.

27. RBI issues currency through __ system?
Ans: Minimum Reserve system.

28. Name the portal launched by RBI to check notes. (ie to know your bank notes)
Ans: PEHCHANO PAISE KI BOLI KYUKI PAISA BOLTA HAI

29. What are the operations of RBI?
Ans: Monetary policy, Currency issuer, Regulates credit and currency system

30. What are the reports that are published by the Reserve bank of India?
Ans: There are various forms of reports published by RBI starting from Annually, half yearly, quarterly to weekly. Let's have a look at them.
1. Annual report
2. Report on Trend and Progress of Banking in India
3. Lectures
4. Report on Currency and Finance
5. Handbook of Statistics on the Indian Economy
6. State Finances: A Study of Budgets
7. Statistical Tables relating to Banks in India
8. Basic Statistical Returns

Half-yearly Publications
1. Monetary Policy Report
2. Financial Stability Report

Quarterly Publications
1. Quarterly Statistics on Deposits and Credit of Scheduled Commercial Banks

Monthly Publications
1. RBI Bulletin
2. Monetary and Credit Information Review

Weekly Publications
1. Weekly Statistical Supplement to the RBI Bulletin

Occasional Publications
1.Occasional Papers
2. DRG Studies. Development Research Group (DRG) is a forum that institutionalizes participation of external expertise in in-house research.

Others:
1.Database on Indian Economy

Data-releases on Survey/Census Results
1.Inflation Expectation Survey of households (IESH)
2. Consumer Confidence survey (CCS),
3. Industrial Outlook survey (IOS),
4. Order book, Inventory and Capacity utilization survey (OBICUS)
5. Survey of Professional Forecasters (SPF).

31. The governor of the Reserve Bank of India is a member of the _____ headed by National Security Advisor Ajit Doval, which is a crucial wing of the National Security Council.
Ans: Strategic Policy Group

32. Name the longest serving RBI Governor?
Ans: Sir Benegal Rama Rau was the longest-serving governor, holding office for over seven years.

33. Name the shortest serving RBI Governor?
Ans: Amitav Ghosh, 20-day term is the shortest.

34. Dr Manmohan Singh, who has handled the post of RBI Governor, Financial Secretary of India and Prime Minister of India was RBI's _____ governor?
Ans: fifteenth governor,

35. How many Training Establishments are there with the Reserve Bank of India?
Ans: Eight training establishments
1. College of Agricultural Banking (CAB): Pune, Maharashtra
2. RBI Academy: Central Office, Mumbai, Maharashtra
3. Reserve Bank Staff College: Chennai, Tamil Nadu
4. Institute for Development and Research in Banking Technology: Hyderabad
5. Centre For Advanced Financial Research and Learning (CAFRAL): Mumbai, Maharashtra
6. Indira Gandhi Institute of Development Research: Mumbai, Maharashtra
7. Indian Institute of Bank Management: Guwahati, Assam
8. National Institute of Bank Management: Pune, Maharashtra

36. Out of eight how many Training Establishments are part of the Reserve Bank?
Ans: Three (RBI Academy, College of Agricultural Banking and Reserve Bank of India Staff College)

37. Out of eight, how many Training Establishments are Autonomous institutions?
Ans: one (Institute for Development and Research in Banking Technology (IDRBT)

38. Out of eight, how many Training Establishments are partially and overall funded by the RBI?
Ans: Four {Centre for Advanced Financial Research and Learning (CAFRAL), Indira Gandhi Institute of Development Research (IGIDR), Indian Institute of Bank Management (IIBM), National Institute of Bank Management (NIBM)}

39. Among the four, how many Training Establishments are fully funded by the RBI?
Ans: Two {Centre for Advanced Financial Research and Learning (CAFRAL), Indira Gandhi Institute of Development Research (IGIDR)}

40. The Reserve Bank of India performs the supervisory function under the guidance of which Board?
Ans: Board for Financial Supervision (BFS).

What is the Board for Financial Supervision?
Ans: The Board was constituted in November 1994 as a committee of the Central Board of Directors of the Reserve Bank of India under the Reserve Bank of

India (Board for Financial Supervision) Regulations, 1994.

The primary objective of BFS is to undertake consolidated supervision of the financial sector comprising Scheduled Commercial and Co-operative Banks, All India Financial Institutions, Local Area Banks, Small Finance Banks, Payments Banks, Credit Information Companies, Non-Banking Finance Companies and Primary Dealers.

41. Who is empowered to control the expansion of bank credit?
Ans: Reserve Bank of India

42. RBI has launched a portal to curb illegal money pooling by firms called?
Ans: Sanchet.rbi.org.in

EVALUATION OF BANKS BY RBI

The four parameters on which banks are supervised in India are:
a. Soundness
b. Financial Efficiency
c. Managerial Efficiency
d. Operational Efficiency

This is done on the basis of an international model known as CAMELS which is applicable to all banks except foreign banks.

CAMELS means:
C: Capital Adequacy
A: Asset Quality
M: Management Quality
E: Earning Ability
L: Liquidity
S: Systems and Controls

For foreign banks in India the rating model is a modified version called CACS.

CACS means:
C: Capital Adequacy
A: Asset Quality
C: Compliance
S: Systems and Controls

RESERVE BANK OF INDIA ACT 1934

1. Name the section of the Reserve Bank of India Act, 1934 that defines Business of RBI?
Ans: Section 17

2. Name the section of the Reserve Bank of India Act, 1934 that defines "Deals with Emergency loans to Banks".
Ans: Section 18

3. Name the section of the Reserve Bank of India Act, 1934 that defines "only RBI has the exclusive rights to issue currency notes in India".
Ans: Section 22

4. Name the section of the Reserve Bank of India Act, 1934 that defines "maximum denomination a note can be Rs. 10,000".
Ans: Section 24

5. Name the section of the Reserve Bank of India Act, 1934 that defines "Describes the legal tender character of Indian bank notes".
Ans: Section 26

6. Name the section of the Reserve Bank of India Act, 1934 that defines "Allows the RBI to form rules regarding the exchange of damaged and imperfect notes".
Ans: Section 28

7. Name the section of the Reserve Bank of India Act, 1934 that defines "In India only the RBI or the central government can issue and accept promissory notes that are payable on demand".
Section 31

8. Name the section of the Reserve Bank of India Act, 1934 that defines "Every scheduled bank must have an average daily balance with the RBI".
Ans: Section 42(1)

9. When was the RBI Act enacted?
Ans: 6th March 1934

MONETARY POLICY OF RBI:

What is meant by monetary policy?

Ans: Monetary policy is the process by which the monetary authority of a country, generally the central bank, controls the supply of money in the economy by its control over interest rates in order to maintain price stability and achieve high economic growth. The Reserve Bank of India is authorized to make monetary policy under the Reserve Bank of India Act, 1934.

Primary functions of Monetary Policy:
1. Adjusting inflation
2. Maintaining price stability
3. Regulating the supply of money
4. Helps in formulating the contraction or expansion of economy.
5. Maintaining high employment
6. Maintaining stable and faster growth
7. Maintaining a good foreign exchange

Instruments of Monetary Policy

Repo rate, Reverse Repo rate, Liquidity Adjustment Facility (LAF), Marginal Standing Facility (MSF), Bank Rate, Cash Reserve Ratio (CRR), Statutory Liquidity Ratio (SLR), Open Market Operations (OMOs), Market Stabilization Scheme (MSS)

Cash Reserve Ratio (CRR): (Generally at 4 %), CRR is the minimum percentage of deposit of the commercial banks that they need to deposit with the RBI.

Situations:

When CRR Increased: Commercial banks need to deposit more money with the RBI. Therefore, less money with Banks to offer loans, loans become dearer with higher interest rates, so people have less money to spend, less demand for goods and services, low prices. Therefore, it the tool to control inflation. Higher CRR sucks money from the economy.

If CRR Decreased: Lower CRR releases more money in the economy.

Statutory Liquidity Ratio (SLR): (Generally at 20-21%), It is the percentage of deposit and liabilities that commercial banks need to keep with them in the form of cash, gold or government approved securities.

Situations:

If SLR increases: Banks need to keep more funds with themselves, they will offer less funds to people, less money in the hands of people, lower demand for goods and services, lower prices.

If SLR decreases: Banks will have more funds with themselves, they will offer more funds to people, more money in people's hand, more demand for goods and services, higher prices.

Repo Rate (Repurchase Agreement): (Generally 6-7%), It is the rate at which RBI lends money to the commercial banks against securities in case banks shortfall in funds. (Banks borrow funds from RBI at a certain rate called Repo rate). (Banks borrow funds in a way of selling Government securities with an agreement of repurchase them at future)

Situations:

If RBI increases Repo rate: It becomes costly for the banks to borrow money from RBI so they in turn hike the rates at which customers borrow money from the banks.

This is to discourage customers from taking loans. It decreases supply of money in markets. Less money with Banks to offer loans, loans become dearer with higher interest rates, so people have less money to spend, less demand for goods and services, low prices. Therefore, it the tool to control inflation.

If RBI decreases Repo rate: It becomes cheaper for the banks to borrow money from RBI so they in turn lower the rates at which customers borrow money from the banks.

This is to encourage customers from taking loans. It increases supply of money in markets. More money with Banks to offer loans, loans become cheaper with lower interest rates, so people have more money to spend, more demand for goods and services, high prices.

Reverse Repo Rate: It is the rate at which RBI borrows money from the commercial banks. (Central bank or RBI takes loans from commercial banks at a interest rate called Reverse Repo Rate.

Situations:
Increases in RRR: Banks will keep more money with RBI, supply of money in market decrease. Price falls.
Decrease in RRR: Banks will keep less money with RBI, supply of money in market increase. Price high.

Bank Rate: it is the rate at which RBI lends money to the commercial banks without any securities.

Marginal Standing Facility (MSF): By this mechanism Commercial banks can get loans in cash from RBI against government securities for their emergency needs. Commercial banks can take loans only up to 1% of their liabilities and time deposits.

Open Market Operation: Buying and Selling Government Securities and Bonds in order to manage liquidity in the economy.

Situations:
Impact of purchasing more Securities by the RBI: More money in the economy-more demand-higher growth rate.
Impact of selling more Securities by the RBI: less money in the economy-less demand-less growth rate.

Some Questions:

1. What happens when CRR is increased?
A. It decreases money supply
B. It increases demand for money
C. It decreases inflation
D. All of the above (Answer)

2. Which of the following counts under SLR?
A. Cash in Hand
B. Gold owned by the bank
C. Balance with RBI
D. All of the above (Answer)

3. What do we call the rate at which the Reserve Bank of India lends money to commercial banks?
A. Repo rate (Answer)
B. Reverse repo rate
C. CRR
D. SLR

4. What is meant by Repo Rate?
Ans: Repo rate is the rate at which RBI lends to its clients generally against government securities.

5. An increase in Repo Rate can
Ans: Increase the cost of borrowing and lending of the banks

6. What is the CRR?
Ans: Cash reserve ratio is a certain percentage of bank deposits which banks are required to keep with RBI in the form of reserves or balances.

7. Which of the following statements is true of SLR?
Ans: Statutory liquidity ratio is to be kept in a non-cash form such as G-secs precious metals, approved securities like bonds. Every financial institution has to maintain this in the number of liquid assets.

MONETARY POLICY COMMITTEE

1.What is Monetary Policy Committee?
Ans: A committee constituted by the Central Government and led by the Governor of RBI with a sole function of fixing the policy instruments interest rate in order to restrain inflation, providing high growth and faster employment. Monetary Policy Committee (MPC) was constituted as per Section 45ZB under the RBI Act of 1934 by the Central Government. Earlier prior to the formation of the committee decisions were taken by the RBI governor alone. MPC conducts meetings quarterly in every year.

2. When did the monetary Policy Committee come into force?
Ans: The monetary Policy Committee came into force on 27th June 2016.

3. Which Committee first proposed the idea for the formation of a five-member Monetary Policy Committee?
Ans: Urijit Patel Committee

4. Which department of RBI assists the MPC in formulation of the policy?
Ans: Monetary Policy Department (MPD)

5. When did the first meeting of MPC was conducted and where?
Ans: 3rd October 2016 in Mumbai.

6. Monetary Policy Committee (MPC) formulates rules and regulations of the Monterey policy of the RBI. MPC was formed under which Act?
Ans: RBI Act 1934

7. The MPC is required to meet at least how many times in a year?
Ans: four (the meeting are head quarterly)

8. How many members form a quorum for a meeting of the MPC?

Ans: four

9. In order to finalise policy MPC members are required to vote, and each member of the MPC has one vote but in the event of equality of votes who can cast the second vote?
Ans: Governor of the RBI

10. The Reserve Bank is required to publish a document once every six months to explain the sources of inflation and the forecasts of inflation for 6-18 months ahead. The documents are called?
Ans: Monetary Policy Report

11. The Monetary Policy Committee consists of the following six members.
1. Monetary Policy Committee (MPC) Chairperson (Governor of the RBI)
2. In-charge of Monetary Policy
3. Member 1
4. Member 2
5. Member 3
6. Member 4

Some Questions:

1.Who is the chairperson of the Monetary Policy Committee of India?
Ans: RBI Governor

2. What do we call the instruments of monetary policy which directly affect the quantity of money supply?
Ans: Quantitative instruments

4. Who is the Central monetary policy Authority in India?
Ans: RBI

OTHER FINANCIAL POLICIES BY RBI

1. Reserve Bank of India (RBI) can increase or reduced the Ways and Means Advances (WMA) for states and Union Territories.

What are Ways and Means Advances?

Ans: WMAs are temporary advances (in simple words loan/lending) given by the RBI to the government (state/center) to tide over any mismatch in receipts and payments.

The WMA scheme was introduced in 1997 and as per Section 17(5) of the RBI Act, 1934. Also, repayment should be made within three months from the date of the making of the advance and the interest charged is basically the present repo rate.

If WMA exceeds 90 days, it would be treated as an overdraft (the interest rate on overdrafts is 2 percentage points more than the repo rate).

2. What is Joint Lenders Forum (JLF)?

Ans: It is basically directing the banks not to break any rules and to meet all the deadlines failing would attract a monetary penalty. JLFs are meetings held to revitalize stressed assets.

Committee formed in the Banking sector And Banking Reforms during 1991 New Economic Policy:

1.Name the committees formed for the Reforms of the Banking Sector?

Ans: The committees formed for the Reforms of the Banking Sector are:

1. Narasimhan Committee report (1)-1991
2. Narasimhan Committee report (2)-1998
3. Nachiket Mor Committee 2013.
4. P J Nayak Committee.

2. Name the Nachiket Mor Committee 2013?

Ans: The Committee on Comprehensive Financial Services for Small Businesses and Low-Income Households, set up by the RBI.

3. What are the Recommendations of Narasimhan Committee Report prepared in 1991.

Ans: The reforms are:

1.Lower SLR

2. Four-tier hierarchy

3. Supervisory functions by RBI sponsored body.

4. Competition

5. Asset Reconstruction fund for recovery of loans.

6. Abolition of branch licensing policy.

6. Proper classification of assets and full disclosure of accounts of banks and financial institutions.

4. On the recommendations of Narasimhan Committee, what measures have been undertaken by government since 1991?

Ans: The following measures are:

1.Lowering SLR and CRR

2. Bringing transparency and professionalism in commercial banks.

3. 100% provision for all Non-performing Assets (NPAs).

4. Under the Capital Adequacy Norms (CAN) the Capital Adequacy ratio was made fixed for all banks. is the ratio of minimum capital to risk asset ratio. In April 1992 RBI fixed CAN at 8%. By March 1996, all public sector banks had attained the ratio of 8%. It was also attained by foreign banks.

5. Interest Rates were deregulated and maintained as per market forces.

6. Banking is open to the private sector.

7. Access To Capital Market: The Banking Companies (Acquisition and Transfer of Undertakings) Act was amended to enable the banks to raise capital through public issues. This is subject to the provision that the holding of Central Government would not fall below 51% of paid-up-capital. SBI has already raised a substantial amount of funds through equity and bonds.

8. Freedom of Operation: Scheduled Commercial Banks are given freedom to open new branches and upgrade extension counters, after attaining capital adequacy ratio and prudential accounting norms. The banks are also permitted to close non-viable branches other than in rural areas.

9. Local Area Banks (LABs): In 1996, RBI issued guidelines for setting up of Local Area Banks, and it gave Its approval for setting up of 7 LABs in private sector. LABs will help in mobilizing rural savings and in channeling them into investment in local areas.

10. Supervision of Commercial Banks: The RBI has set up a Board of Financial Supervision with an advisory Council to strengthen the supervision of banks and financial institutions. In 1993, RBI established a new department known as Department of Supervision as an independent unit for supervision of commercial banks.

11. Recovery of Debts: The Government of India passed the "Recovery of debts due to Banks and Financial Institutions Act 1993" in order to facilitate and speed up the recovery of debts due to banks and financial institutions. Six Special Recovery Tribunals have been set up. An Appellate Tribunal has also been set up in Mumbai.

BANKING REGULATION ACT 1949

1. Name legislation in India that regulates all banking firms in India.
Ans: The Banking Regulation Act, 1949

2. The Banking Regulation Act, 1949 was passed as?
Ans: Banking Companies Act 1949. Banking Companies Act 1949 came into force from 16 March 1949

3. The Banking Companies Act 1949 changed to Banking Regulation Act 1949 on?
Ans: 1 March 1966.

4. When was the Banking Regulation Act, 1949 applicable in J&K?
Ans: 1956

4. Initially, Banking Companies Act 1949 was applicable only to banking companies. But in which year was it amended to make it applicable to cooperative banks and to introduce other changes?
Ans: 1965.

5. In which year, it was amended to bring the cooperative banks under the supervision of the Reserve Bank of India?
Ans: 2020

6. Facts of Banking Companies Act 1949.
Ans: It helps in:
1.providing a framework under which commercial banking in India is supervised and regulated.
2. Primary Agricultural Credit Society and cooperative land mortgage banks are excluded from the Act.
3. The Act gives Reserve Bank of India (RBI) the power to license banks, have regulation over shareholding and voting rights of shareholders; supervise the appointment of the boards and management; regulate the operations of banks; lay down instructions for audits; control moratorium, mergers and liquidation; issue directives in the interests of public good and on banking policy, and impose penalties.

BANKING NATIONALIZATION

We will understand the concept of bank nationalization with an example. Consider a single parent. Let us name her Ms Sharma. She has two children, one boy and one girl. Both are raised in a friendly, loving and caring environment at home. Ms Sharma ensures that her children get all the necessary education and nourishment which they deserve and takes utmost care in their upbringing. In the neighborhood, few homeless kids live across the street. They, however, are not well brought up and make their living by doing odd jobs or sometimes even by indulging in activities which may not be ethically correct. Hence, one day Ms Sharma decides to adopt two such kids from the neighborhood who are homeless. She brings them to her own home, enrolls them into school, teaches them good habits and morals and also looks after their nourishment. Thus, in this analogy: Ms Sharma is the government. Her kids are public sector banks. The "adopted" kids are nationalized banks. Nationalized banks are those who were private sector banks but later brought under the control of the government. Public sector banks are those banks in which the government already has a majority of stakes (more than 50%).

To many of us, both 'public sector bank' and 'nationalized bank' might not seem so different but there are a few notable differences between them.

Public Sector Banks: Public sector banks are under the government as the government is a major stakeholder of these banks. There are 12 public sector banks in India. Public sector banks also include nationalized banks because every nationalized bank is, or will become a public sector bank.

A public sector bank is a bank in which the majority stakeholder is the government. Nationalized banks are also public sector banks.

Public sector banks include all the nationalized banks in them as it is a broader term.

These banks start as banks under the state government or the central government. Punjab National Bank, Bank of Baroda, Central Bank of India, State Bank of India, etc.

Nationalized Banks: A nationalized bank is the one that started as a private sector bank but was later taken by the government for betterment.

A nationalized bank is the one that starts as a private sector bank or under the ownership of someone but is later taken under the government through some kind of ordinance for the good of the nation.

These banks start as private sector banks or under the ownership of someone. UCO Bank, Union Bank of India, Dena Bank, etc.

In Common Sense: Both Public Sector banks and nationalized banks come under the category of commercial banks in India.

What is a Public Sector Bank?
A public sector bank is the one in which the majority shareholder (more than 50%) is the government and the government is responsible for all the activities that occur in it. The nationalized banks are also public sector banks. There are currently 12 public sector banks in India. They are:
Punjab National Bank
Bank of Baroda
Bank of India
Central Bank of India
Canara Bank
Union Bank of India
Indian Overseas Bank
Punjab and Sind Bank
Indian Bank
UCO Bank
Bank of Maharashtra
State Bank of India

INDIAN CURRENCY SYSTEM & RESERVE BANK OF INDIA

About Indian Currency notes and Coins

1. The issuance of the currency in India is controlled by ____.
Ans: Reserve Bank of India on the basis of the Reserve Bank of India Act, 1934.

2. Rupee was prior known by rupiya-the silver coin weighing 178 grains minted in northern India between 1540 and 1545 during Mughal empire. Who has named it?
Ans: By first Sher Shah Suri.

3. The Government of India introduced its first paper money on?
Ans: In 1861,
₹10 note in 1864, ₹5 note in 1872, ₹10,000 note in 1899, ₹100 note in 1900, ₹50 note in 1905, ₹500 note in 1907 and ₹1,000 note in 1909. In 1917, ₹1 and ₹2 and 8 Annas notes were introduced.

4. The Reserve Bank of India began banknote production in which year?
Ans: 1938

5. After India's independence new designs of currency notes were introduced to replace the portrait of which British king?
Ans: George VI.

6. All pre-independence banknotes were officially demonetized on __?
Ans: 28 April 1957.

7. After independence Rs 500 notes were introduced on
Ans: 1987

8. After independence Rs 1000 notes were introduced on
Ans: 2000

9. The Mahatma Gandhi Series of banknotes were introduced in 1996 replacing the series of ____.
Ans: Lion Capital

10. The first notes with Mahatma Gandhi series was.
Ans: Rs 10 and Rs 500

11. The Indian currency is Pegged with Bhutanese ngultrum (at par) and ___ country's currency.
Ans: Nepalese rupee (higher value)

12. In which year new rupee sign (₹) was officially adopted.
Ans: 2010, a new rupee sign (₹) was officially adopted.

13. The first series of coins with the new rupee sign started in circulation on ___.
Ans: 8 July 2011.

14. The new '₹' sign has been incorporated into banknotes of the Mahatma Gandhi Series in denominations of ₹10, ₹20, ₹50, ₹100, ₹500 and ₹1,000 on ____.
Ans: January 2012.

15. On which date the Government of India announced the demonetization of ₹500 and ₹1,000 banknotes?
Ans: 8 November 2016

16. After demonetization in 2016 the newly redesigned series of ₹500 banknotes, in addition to a new denomination of ₹2,000 banknote started circulation since ____.
Ans: 10 November 2016.

17. The new ₹2,000 banknote has a magenta base colour, with a portrait of Mahatma Gandhi as well as the Ashoka Pillar Emblem on the front. But in the back side there is a motif of ___ depicting the country's first venture into interplanetary space.
Ans: Mars Orbiter Mission (MOM), Mangalyan

The new ₹500 banknote has a stone-grey base colour with an image of the Red Fort along with the Indian flag printed on the back.

The new ₹200 banknote has an orange base colour with an image of the Sanchi stupa printed on the back.

The new ₹100 banknote has a lavender base colour with an image of the Rani ki vav printed on the back.

The new ₹50 banknote has a cyan colour with an image of the hampi with chariot printed on the back.

The new ₹20 banknote has a yellow colour with an image of the Ellora caves printed on the back.

The new ₹10 banknote has a brown colour with an image of the Sun Temple Konark printed on the back.

The new ₹5 banknote has a green colour with an image of the Tractor printed on the back.

18. The new Indian banknote series features a few micro printed texts on various locations. The texts are.
Ans: "RBI", "भारत" and "INDIA" respectively.

19. Coins of the Indian rupee (INR) were first minted in ____.
Ans: 1950.

Today, circulating coins exist in denominations of One Rupee, Two Rupees, Five Rupees, Ten Rupees and Twenty Rupees.

20. Coins up to 50 paise are called ____.
Ans: small coins

21. Coins of Rupee one and above are called ____.
Ans: Rupee Coins

22. The Government of India has the sole right to design and mint coins in various denominations under which act?

Ans: Coinage Act, 2011 (amended)

Coins are minted at the four India Government Mints at Mumbai, Alipore (Kolkata), Saifabad (Hyderabad), Cherlapally (Hyderabad) and NOIDA (UP).

23. Coins can be issued up to the denomination of how much rupees as per the Coinage Act, 2011.
Ans: Rs.1000

24. The first Indian commemorative coin was issued in which year in remembrance of Jawaharlal Nehru's birth anniversary.
Ans: The first Indian commemorative coin was issued in **1964** in remembrance of Jawaharlal Nehru. These coins, released in denominations of 1 Rupee and 50 Paise shortly after his death, featured a bust of Nehru and marked a significant moment in Indian numismatic history.

25. The first ever Coin Mint established in India was ____.
Ans: Kolkata Mint, established in 1757. Latest being the Noida Mint was in 1988.

26. How much currency to be produced?
Ans: The Reserve Bank decides the volume and value of banknotes (except Re. 1 note) depending on the requirement in order to maintain inflation, GDP growth, replacement of soiled banknotes, etc.

27. Who decides the issue of coin?
Ans: The Government of India decides the quantity of coins to be minted on the basis of indents (official order) received from the Reserve Bank.

28. How does the Reserve Bank estimate the demand for banknotes?
The Reserve Bank estimates the demand for banknotes on the basis of the growth rate of the economy, demand of growth and supply and other statistical measures.

29. What is a currency chest?

Ans: In order to facilitate proper distribution of notes and coins, the Reserve Bank of India has authorized some selected bank branches to store banknotes and coins on their behalf, these branches are known as Currency Chests.

30. What is a small coin depot?
Ans: In order to stock coins, some bank branches are also authorized to establish Small Coin Depots, and these Small Coin Depots are responsible to distribute small coins when needed.

31. What are soiled, mutilated and imperfect banknotes?
Ans: Soiled note: Dirty note due to usage or two piece note pasted together.
Mutilated banknote: A portion of the note is missing or composed of more than two pieces.
Imperfect banknote: Any banknote, which is wholly or partially, obliterated, shrunk, washed, altered or indecipherable but does not include a mutilated banknote.

32. Can soiled and mutilated banknotes be exchanged for value?
Ans: Yes. Such banknotes can be exchanged for value.

34. Clean Note Policy: Under this policy Reserve Bank of India directs users:
a) Not to staple the banknotes
b) Not to write / put a rubber stamp or any other mark.

35. The Reserve Bank has the sole right to issue every currency note. Yes or No?
Ans: No, except one rupee note which is issued by the Ministry of Finance,

36. Re Note 1 has been released in the country and it bears the signature of ____.
Ans: Finance Secretary of India

37. RBI follows a minimum reserve system in the note issue. Initially, it used to keep 40 percent of gold reserves in its total assets.
But, since 1957, it has to maintain how much amount of Gold and foreign exchange reserves?
Ans: Rs. 200 cores of gold of which gold reserves should be of the value of Rs. 115 crores.

38. During the British period the one rupee note was used as a currency in Persian and Gulf countries. Name the countries?
Ans: Dubai, Muscat and Oman

39. The one rupee note inspired the Portuguese to issue one rupee notes in which place of India?
Ans: Their colony Goa and even the French to start the French 'Roupie' in 1919.

40. Which bank note is the only denomination note with the text "Government of India" printed on it whereas all other currencies have 'Bharatiya Reserve Bank' and 'Reserve Bank of India' printed on them?
Ans: One rupee notes

41. What are the different types of Money?
Ans: The different types of money are:

a. Commodity Money - Commodity money value is derived from the commodity out of which it is made. The commodity itself represents money, and the money is the commodity. For instance, commodities that have been used a Medium of
exchanges include gold, silver, copper, salt, peppercorns, rice, large stones, etc.

b. Representative Money - Representative money is the money that includes token coins, or any other physical tokens like certificates, that can be reliably exchanged for a fixed amount/quantity of a commodity like gold or silver.

c. Fiat Money - Fiat money, also known as fiat currency is the money whose value is not derived from any intrinsic value or any guarantee that it can be converted into valuable commodities (like gold).

Instead, it derives value only based On government order (fiat).

d. Commercial Bank Money - Commercial bank money or the demand deposits are claims against financial institutions which can be used for purchasing goods and services.

42. Money supply of RBI: The RBI calculates total money supply in the economy on the basis of Monetary Aggregates.

M0: Reserve money also known as 'H' [High Powered Money]. It is created by the Central Bank of the country.
M1: Narrow money i.e., Total Money Supply in a short period. It is Currency with the public + Demand Deposits (DD) + Other deposits with the RBI.
M2: M1 + Time Liabilities Portion of DD + Certificate of deposits + Time deposits maturing within/upto 1 year.
M3: M2 + Time Deposits maturing after 1 year + Call borrowing by banks from non-depository financial corporations.

STRUCTURE OF BANKING IN INDIA

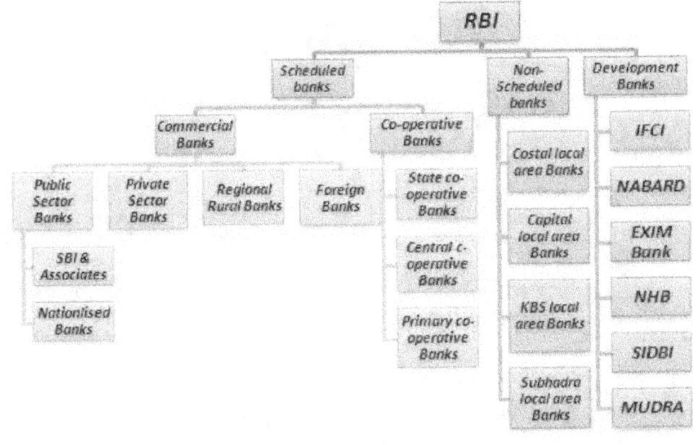

Central Bank: The central bank is the financial administrator that regulates the banking sector of a country. In India it's The Reserve Bank of India. The primary functions of the central bank are:

a. Supervision and administration of the financial system.
b. Implementing monetary policies
c. Guiding other banks is the reason it is known as banker's bank.
d. Issuing currency
e. Supervisor of the financial system

Scheduled Banks and Non-Scheduled Banks
Scheduled Banks: Scheduled banks are covered under the 2nd Schedule of the Reserve Bank of India Act, 1934.

Non-Scheduled Banks: Banks which are not covered under this 2nd Schedule of the Reserve Bank of India Act 1934 are called Non-Scheduled Banks

There are two main categories of Scheduled banks in India namely Scheduled Commercial banks, Scheduled Cooperative banks

Commercial Banks: Organized under the Banking Companies Act, 1956. They operate on a commercial basis and its main objective is profit. They have a unified structure and are owned by the government, state, or any private entity. They tend to all sectors ranging from rural to urban. These banks do not charge concessional interest rates unless instructed by the RBI. Public deposits are the main source of funds for these banks.

Co-operative Banks: Co-operative banks are registered under the Cooperative Societies Act, 1912 and they are run by an elected managing committee. These work on a no-profit no-loss basis and mainly serve entrepreneurs, small businesses, industries and self-employment in urban areas. In rural areas, they mainly finance agriculture-based activities like farming, livestock and hatcheries.

Its Types: Urban Co-operative Banks & State Co-operative Banks
Urban Co-operative Banks refer to the primary cooperative banks located in urban and semi-urban

areas. These banks essentially lent to small borrowers and businesses centered around communities, localities workplace groups.

According to the RBI, on 31st March, 2003 there were 2,104 Urban Co-operative Banks of which 56 were scheduled banks. About 79% of these are located in five states, – Andhra Pradesh, Gujarat, Karnataka, Maharashtra and Tamil Nadu.

State Co-operative Banks: A State Cooperative Bank is a federation of the central cooperative bank which acts as custodian of the cooperative banking structure in the State.

Banks can also be classified on the basis of Scheduled and Non-Scheduled Banks. It is essential for every individual to check if they are holding their savings or deposit account with a Scheduled Bank or Non-Scheduled Bank. Scheduled Banks are also covered under the depositor insurance program of Deposit Insurance and Credit Guarantee Corporation (DICGC), which is beneficial for all the account holders holding a savings and fixed / recurring deposit account. Under DICGC, bank deposits of up to Rs 1 lakh, including the fixed, savings, current and recurring deposits, per depositor per bank in the event of bank failure are insured.

Cooperative Banks: Cooperative Banks are governed under the law enacted by the ___ government?
Ans: state

What is the primary purpose or function of Cooperative banks?
Ans: Principal purpose is to enhance social welfare by providing low-interest loans.

Cooperative Banks are arranged in a ___ tier system.
Ans: Three

Name the three-tiered system of Cooperative Banks?
Ans: Tier-1: State Cooperative Banks, (State Level)
(regulated by RBI, State Govt, NABARD)
The state owns the company, and the senior management is chosen by the members.

Tier-2: Central/District Cooperative Banks, (District Level)
Tier-3: Primary Agriculture Cooperative Banks, (Village Level)

Scheduled commercial Banks are further divided into 4 types as below -
1. Public sector banks -> SBI and its Associates and other Nationalized banks.
2. Private sector Banks
3. Regional Rural Banks
4. Foreign Banks

Scheduled Co-operative banks are further divided into 2 types, namely -
Scheduled State Co-operative banks
Scheduled Urban Co-operative banks

Public Sector Banks: These are nationalized banks and account for more than 75 percent of the total banking business in the country. Majority of stakes in these banks are held by the government. In terms of volume, SBI is the largest public sector bank in India and after its merger with its 5 associate banks (as on 1st April 2017) it has got a position among the top 50 banks of the world. There are a total of 12 nationalized banks in the country.

What are Government Banks
The public sector banks or PSBs are more commonly known as Government Banks. The government banks are not under the direct control of the government, but the Government of India is the majority stakeholder in them i.e the GOI has more than 51% of the shares. There are 12 government banks in India or Public sector banks.

Public sector Banks – A bank where the majority stakes are owned by the Government or the central bank of the country.

Private Sector Banks: These include banks in which major stake or equity is held by private shareholders. All the banking rules and regulations laid down by the

RBI will be applicable on private sector banks as well. Given below is the list of private-sector banks in India- HDFC, ICICI, AXIS BANK

Private sector Banks – A bank where the majority stakes are owned by a private organization or an individual or a group of people

Foreign Banks: A foreign bank is one that has its headquarters in a foreign country but operates in India as a private entity. These banks are under obligation to follow the regulations of its home country as well as the country in which they are operating.

Foreign Banks are basically the banks with their headquarters in foreign countries and branches in our country, fall under this type of bank

Regional Rural Banks (RRB)

1. The RRB was formed on?

2nd oct 1975 under the Regional Rural Bank Act of 1976.

2. How much % of RRB are owned by the Government of India?

Government of India (50%), Nationalized Banks (35%), State Governments (15%)

3. How many RRBs were set up on 2 October 1975 on the recommendations of the Narsimha Committee on Rural Credit, during the tenure of Indira Gandhi's government.

Five

4. Name the first RRB of India?

Prathama Bank, with head office in Moradabad, Uttar Pradesh was the first RRB. (Sponsored by Syndicate Bank and had an authorised capital of Rs. 5 crore).

The other four RRBs were Gaur Gramin Bank (sponsored by UCO Bank), Gorakhpur Kshetriya Gramin Bank (sponsored by State Bank of India), Haryana Kshetriya Gramin Bank (sponsored by Punjab National Bank), and Jaipur-Nagpur Anchalik Gramin Bank (sponsored by UCO Bank).

5. Name the committee that was constituted in September 2009 to analyse the financials of the RRBs and suggest measures, including re-capitalisation to bring the CRAR of RRBs to at least 9% in a sustainable manner by 2012.

K C Chakrabarty committee, the deputy governor of the Reserve Bank of India (RBI).

6. The purpose of which type of banks was to include rural areas into the economic mainstream since around 70% of the Indian population was rural?

RRBs

Non-Scheduled Banks:

Local Area Banks (LAB)

1.In India, Local Area Banks (LAB) was first introduced in which year?

Ans: 1996.

2. Which Sector organizes Local Area Banks (LAB)?

Ans: The private sector.

3. The primary goal of Local Area Banks is?

Ans: To make a profit.

4. Local Area Banks are governed under __?

Ans: The 1956 Companies Act.

Payments Banks:

1.The concept of Payments Banks is brought in by ____?

Ans: Reserve Bank of India.

The concept of Payments Banks was introduced by the Reserve Bank of India (RBI) in **2014**, based on recommendations from the Nachiket Mor Committee which submitted its report in January 2014.

2. People with an account in the payments bank can only deposit an amount up to Rs _____?

Ans: Rs.1,00,000/-

3. People with an account in the payments bank ________ (can/cannot) apply for loans or credit cards under the account.
Ans: Cannot

4. Other facilities of payment banks include.
Ans: online banking, mobile banking, the issue of ATM, and debit cards.

5. The list of payments banks in our country: Airtel Payments Bank, India Post Payments Bank, Fino Payments Bank, Jio Payments Bank, Paytm Payments Bank, NSDL Payments Bank.

Payments Bank
1. Airtel Payments Bank established in 2017, New Delhi, Delhi (First Payment Bank)
2. India Post Payments Bank established in 2018, New Delhi,
3. Paytm Payments Bank was established in 2017, Noida, Uttar Pradesh
4. Jio Payments Bank established in 2018, Mumbai, Maharashtra
5. Fino Payments Bank established in 2017, Mumbai, Maharashtra
6. NSDL Payments Bank established in 2018, Mumbai, Maharashtra
7. Aditya Birla Payments Bank – Headquartered in Mumbai, the payments bank was opened in 2016, but due to lack of funds it shut its business in 2019 and it ceased to be a banking company in July 2020.

Small Finance Banks:
This sort of bank, as the name implies, provides loans and financial help to micro industries, small farmers, and the unorganized sector of society. The country's central bank oversees these institutions.

This is a niche banking segment in the country and is aimed at providing financial inclusion to sections of society that are not served by other banks. The main customers of small finance banks include micro industries, small and marginal farmers, unorganized sector entities and small business units. These are licensed under Section 22 of the Banking Regulation Act, 1949 and are governed by the provisions of RBI Act, 1934 and FEMA.

As the name suggests, this type of bank looks after the micro industries, small farmers, and the unorganized sector of society by providing them with loans and financial assistance. These banks are governed by the central bank of the country.

AU Small Finance Bank, Equitas Small Finance Bank, Jana Small Finance Bank, Northeast Small Finance Bank, Capital Small Finance Bank, Fincare Small Finance Bank, Suryoday Small Finance Bank, Ujjivan Small Finance Bank, Esaf Small Finance Bank, Utkarsh Small Finance Bank.
Committee: Usha Thorat and Nachiketa More

Small Finance Bank:
1. Capital Small Finance Bank, HQ: Jalandhar, Punjab, 2016. (First Small Payment Bank)
2. Ujjivan Small Finance Bank, HQ: Bangalore, Karnataka, 2017
3. Jana Small Finance Bank, 2018, HQ: Bangalore, Karnataka
4. Equitas Small Finance Bank, 2016, HQ: Chennai, Tamil Nadu
5. AU Small Finance Bank, 2017, HQ: Jaipur, Rajasthan
6. Fincare Small Finance Bank, 2017, HQ: Bangalore, Karnataka
7. ESAF Small Finance Bank, 2017, HQ: Thrissur, Kerala
8. Northeast Small Finance Bank, 2017, HQ: Guwahati, Assam
9. Suryoday Small Finance Bank, 2017, HQ: Navi Mumbai, Maharashtra
10. Utkarsh Small Finance Bank, 2018, HQ: Varanasi, Uttar Pradesh
11. Shivalik Small Finance Bank, 2021, HQ: Saharanpur, Uttar Pradesh
12. Unity Small Finance Bank, 2021, Gurugram, Haryana.

BANKS AND BANKING IN INDIA

At present there are 12 public sector banks. (as of 2022)

1.Bank of Baroda
HQ: Vadodara, Gujarat.
The Maharaja of Baroda, Sayajirao Gaekwad III, founded the bank on 20 July 1908 in the Princely State of Baroda, in Gujarat.
Vijaya bank and Dena bank merged into BOB. The merger came into effect on 1 April 2019.

2. Bank of India
Founded: 7 September 1906; 115 years ago
HQ: Mumbai, Maharashtra

3. Bank of Maharashtra
Founded: 16 September 1935; 86 years ago
The bank was founded by V. G. Kale and D. K. Sathe in Pune, India.
HQ: Pune, Maharashtra

4. Canara Bank
Ammembal Subba Rao Pai, a philanthropist, established the Canara Hindu Permanent Fund in Mangalore, India, on 1 July 1906. The bank changed its name to Canara Bank Limited in 1910 when it was incorporated.
HQ: Bengaluru, Karnataka
Syndicate Bank HQ: Manipal. On 1 April 2020, the bank was merged into Canara Bank.

5. Punjab National Bank
HQ: New Delhi

6. Union Bank of India
HQ: Mumbai, Maharashtra

7. UCO Bank
HQ: Kolkata, West Bengal

8. Central Bank of India
HQ: Mumbai, Maharashtra

9. Indian Overseas Bank
HQ: Chennai, Tamil Nadu

10. Punjab and Sind Bank
HQ: New Delhi

11. Indian bank

12. State Bank of India
HQ: Mumbai, Maharashtra
Founded: 1 July 1955

Banks and their Taglines

Major Indian Public Sector Banks & Taglines
State Bank of India (SBI): Pure Banking, Nothing Else, With You – All The Way, The Banker to Every Indian, The Nation Banks on Us, Suraksha aur Bharosa Dono.
Punjab National Bank (PNB): The name you can bank upon
Bank of Baroda: India's International Bank
Canara Bank: Together we can
Union Bank of India: Good people to bank with
Indian Overseas Bank: Good people to grow with
UCO Bank: Honours your trust

Major Indian Private Sector Banks & Taglines
HDFC Bank: We understand your world
ICICI Bank: Hum Hai Na / Khayal Apka
Axis Bank: Dil Se Open / Badhti Ka Naam Zindagi
Kotak Mahindra Bank: Let's make money simple
Yes Bank: Experience our expertise
IndusInd Bank: We Make You Feel Richer
Federal Bank: Your perfect banking partner

International Banks & Taglines
Citibank: The Citi never sleeps
HSBC: Together we thrive
Deutsche Bank: A Passion to Perform
Standard Chartered: Your Right Partner
BNP Paribas: The bank for a changing world

Bank of Calcutta (1806 – 1921), Bank of Bombay: (1840 – 1921), Bank of Madras: (1843 – 1921) are the three Presidency Banks that formed Imperial Bank of India: (1921 – 1955). Which finally formed State Bank of India.

Pursuant to the provisions of the State Bank of India Act of 1955, the Reserve Bank of India, which is India's central bank, acquired a controlling interest in the Imperial Bank of India. On 1 July 1955, the Imperial Bank of India became the State Bank of India. In 2008, the Government of India acquired the Reserve Bank of India's stake in SBI so as to remove any conflict of interest because the RBI is the country's banking regulatory authority.

On 7 October 2013, Arundhati Bhattacharya became the first woman to be appointed Chairperson of the bank.

SBI acquired the control of seven banks in 1960. They were the seven regional banks of former Indian princely states. They were renamed, prefixing them with 'State Bank of'. These seven banks were State Bank of Bikaner and Jaipur (SBBJ), State Bank of Hyderabad (SBH), State Bank of Indore (SBN), State Bank of Mysore (SBM), State Bank of Patiala (SBP), State Bank of Saurashtra (SBS) and State Bank of Travancore (SBT). All these banks were given the same logo as the parent bank, SBI. State Bank of India and all its associate banks used the same blue Keyhole logo said to have been inspired by Ahmedabad's Kankaria Lake.

The plans for making SBI a single very large bank by merging the associate banks started in 2008, and in September the same year, SBS merged with SBI. The very next year, State Bank of Indore (SBN) also merged.

Following a merger process, the merger of the 5 remaining associate banks, (viz. State Bank of Bikaner and Jaipur, State Bank of Hyderabad, State Bank of Mysore, State Bank of Patiala, State Bank of Travancore); and the Bharatiya Mahila Bank) with the SBI was given an in-principle approval by the Union Cabinet on 15 June 2016. This came a month after the SBI board had, on 17 May 2016, cleared a proposal to merge its five associate banks and Bharatiya Mahila Bank with itself.

On 15 February 2017, the Union Cabinet approved the merger of five associate banks with SBI. An analyst foresaw an initial negative impact as a result of different pension liability provisions and accounting policies for bad loans. The merger went into effect from 1 April 2017.

Bharatiya Mahila Bank (BMB; lit. 'Indian Women's Bank') was a fully owned subsidiary of State Bank of India based in Mumbai, India. Former Indian Prime Minister Manmohan Singh inaugurated the system on 19 November 2013 on the occasion of the 96th birth anniversary of former Indian Prime Minister Indira Gandhi. As part of the Modi government's banking reforms and to ensure greater banking outreach to women, the bank merged with State Bank of India on 1 April 2017.
Founded: 19 November 2013
Merged with State Bank of India
Headquarters: Delhi, India
While being run by women, and lending exclusively to women, the bank allowed deposits to flow from everyone. India was the third country, after Pakistan and Tanzania, to have a bank exclusively to benefit women.

Specialized Banks

Certain banks exist just to serve a certain purpose. Specialized banks are the name for several types of financial institutions. These are some of them:

SIDBI (Small Industries Development Bank of India) - SIDBI can provide a loan for a small-scale enterprise or business. With the support of this bank, small businesses can get current technology and equipment. Small Industries Development Bank of

India (SIDBI) is the apex regulatory body for overall licensing and regulation of micro, small and medium enterprise finance companies in India. It is under the jurisdiction of the Ministry of Finance; Government of India headquartered at Lucknow and having its offices all over the country. The SIDBI was established on April 2, 1990, by Government of India, as a wholly owned subsidiary of IDBI Bank. It was delinked from IDBI w.e.f. March 27, 2000. It was established in 1990, through an Act of Parliament.

Export and Import Bank (EXIM Bank) - EXIM Bank stands for Export and Import Bank. This type of bank can provide loans or other financial help to foreign countries that are exporting or importing goods. The Export-Import Bank of India (Exim Bank) is a specialized financial institution in India that was established in 1982. The bank's primary function is to finance, facilitate and promote India's international trade. It is owned by the Government of India and operates as a statutory corporation. Its operations are governed by the Export-Import Bank of India Act, 1981

Founded: 1 January March 1982 (introduced) & 7 April 1982 (received assent of President of India) (under the Export-Import Bank of India Act, 1981)
Founder: Government of India
Headquarters: Mumbai, India

NABARD (National Bank for Agricultural and Rural Development) – People can resort to NABARD for any type of financial support for rural, handicraft, village, and agricultural development. National Bank for Agriculture and Rural Development (NABARD) is an apex regulatory body for overall regulation of regional rural banks and apex cooperative banks in India. It is fully owned by Ministry of Finance, Government of India.
Formation: 12 July 1982;
Type: Regulatory Body
Purpose: Agriculture Development, Rural Development, Credit Planning, Refinance,

Supervision of Regional Rural Banks, Supervision of Apex Cooperative Banks
Headquarters: Mumbai, India
Owner: Ministry of Finance, Government of India

National Housing Bank (NHB) is the apex regulatory body for overall regulation and licensing of housing finance companies in India. It is under the jurisdiction of Ministry of Finance, Government of India. It was set up on 9 July 1988 under the National Housing Bank Act, 1987. Headquarters: New Delhi, India

ECGC Limited (Formerly Export Credit Guarantee Corporation of India Limited) is a government owned export credit agency of India. It is under the ownership of the Ministry of Commerce and Industry, Government of India, and is headquartered in Mumbai, Maharashtra. It is basically an Insurance Industry which was founded in 30 July 1957. It provides export credit insurance support to Indian exporters and banks.

Other specialist banks exist, each with a unique function to play in the financial development of the country.

In India, co-operative banks play a crucial role in rural financing, with funding of areas under agriculture, livestock, milk, personal finance, self-employment, setting up of small-scale units among the few focus points for both urban and rural cooperative banks.

They provide a much-needed alternative to the age-old exploitative practice of people approaching the village moneylender, most often getting into a debt-trap that they struggle to pull themselves out of.

The cooperative banking system came into being with the aim to promote saving and investment habits among people, especially in rural parts of the country.

What are co-operative banks?

Co-operative banks are financial entities established on a co-operative basis and belonging to their members. This means that the customers of a co-operative bank are also its owners. These banks provide a wide range of regular banking and financial services. However, there are some points where they differ from other banks. Broadly, co-operative banks in India are divided into two categories - urban and rural.

Rural cooperative credit institutions could either be short-term or long-term in nature. Further, short-term cooperative credit institutions are further sub-divided into State Co-operative Banks, District Central Co-operative Banks, Primary Agricultural Credit Societies.

Meanwhile, the long-term institutions are either State Cooperative Agriculture and Rural Development Banks (SCARDBs) or Primary Cooperative Agriculture and Rural Development Banks (PCARDBs).

On the other hand, Urban Co-operative Banks (UBBs) are either scheduled or non-scheduled. Scheduled and non-scheduled UCBs are again of two kinds- multi-state and those operating in single state.

Who oversees these banks?
In India, co-operative banks are registered under the States Cooperative Societies Act. They also come under the regulatory ambit of the Reserve Bank of India (RBI) under two laws, namely, the Banking Regulations Act, 1949, and the Banking Laws (Co-operative Societies) Act, 1955. They were brought under the RBI's watch in 1966, a move which brought the problem of dual regulation along with it.

DIFFERENT TYPES OF BANKING

1. Para Banking: In Para Banking, banks organize their activities on a departmental basis or by setting up subsidiaries. This Banking is little different from normal Banking of withdrawal or deposit of money.

2. Narrow Banking: When banks invest most of its money in government bonds and securities in order to avoid risk in the market it is called Narrow Banking.

3. Offshore Banking: This kind of Banking exists when a bank accepts currencies of other countries and provides financial and legal benefits like privacy and minimal taxation.

4. Green Banking: When a bank accepts, promotes and practices clean energy and tries to reduce the carbon footprint from banking activities. This kind of Banking is known as Green Banking.

5. Retail Banking: This is the most popular and normal banking activity where there is direct dealing with the consumers. Also known as consumer banking or personal banking.

6. Wholesale banking: When a bank provides services to the organizations like Mortgage Brokers, corporate clients, medium scale companies, real estate developers and investors, international trade finance businesses, then it is known as Wholesale Banking.

7. Universal Banking: In universal Banking banks are allowed to undertake all types of financial activities under the guidance of RBI, Government and related legal Acts. The concept of universal Banking was brought by R H Khan committee.

8. Islamic Banking: Islamic banking is a kind of banking activity which strictly follows the principles of the Islamic law (Sharia) and its application practically through the development in Islamic economics. A better and more apt term for Islamic banking is Sharia Compliant Finance.

9. Unit Banking: USA is where such type of banking was first introduced. In such a type of banking, all the operations are performed from a single branch. A customer having an account in a specified branch has to undergo all banking activities through that branch.

Examples are Regional Rural Banks and Local Area Banks.

10. Mixed Banking: Mixed banking is a type of banking in which deposits and investment activities take place simultaneously. It can also be described as the dual functioning of investment banking and commercial banking.

11. Chain Banking: Chain banking is a type of banking which is a group of minimum 3 banks held together by a group of people to carry out effective banking activities. Instead of having a holding company the bank functions independently. The revenue is maximized since there is no overlap of activities.

12. Relationship Banking: In such a type of banking, the major needs of the customers are understood by the bank and accordingly banking services are provided to the individual. Banks get to know if the customer is creditworthy since they have to gather information about its customers.

Correspondent Banking: In more than 200 countries, this type of banking is prevalent and is considered the most profitable way of doing business. In such a type of banking, the bank does not have a physical presence or any limitations in the permission of operations. It acts as a banking agent for a home bank.

ACTIVITIES OF BANKING:
1. Accepting Deposits 2. Advancing Loans

1.Accepting Deposits: Banks accept deposits on various types of accounts as opened by the depositor or customer. Therefore the different types of bank accounts in India are:
Whether you are a housewife or a college student, a business owner or a business house, a retired professional or Indian living abroad, not having a bank account is unimaginable. Based on the purpose, frequency of transaction, and location of the account-holder, banks offer a bouquet of bank accounts to

choose from. Here is a list of some of the types of bank accounts in India.

1. Current account
A current account is a deposit account for traders, business owners, and entrepreneurs, who need to make and receive payments more often than others. These accounts hold more liquid deposits with no limit on the number of transactions per day. Current accounts allow overdraft facility, that is withdrawing more than what is currently available in the account. Also, unlike savings accounts, where you earn some interest, these are zero-interest bearing accounts. You need to maintain a minimum balance to be able to operate current accounts.

2. Savings account
A savings bank account is a regular deposit account, where you earn a minimum rate of interest. Here, the number of transactions you can make each month is capped. Banks offer a variety of Savings Accounts based on the type of depositor, features of the product, age or purpose of holding the account, and so on. There are regular savings accounts, savings accounts for children, senior citizens or women, institutional savings accounts, family savings accounts, and so many more.

You have the option to pick from a range of savings products. There are zero-balance savings accounts and also advanced ones with features like auto sweep, debit cards, bill payments and cross-product benefits. A cross-product benefit is when you have a savings account with a bank and get to avail special offers on opening a second account such as a demat account.
Apply for Online Saving Account Opening here, in secure and simple Video Kyc process.
Apply for Savings Account here.

3. Salary account
Among the different types of bank accounts, your salary account is the one you have opened as per the tie-up between your employer and the bank. This is the account, where salaries of every employee are

credited to at the beginning of the pay cycle. Employees can pick their type of salary account based on the features they want. The bank, where you have a salary account, also maintains reimbursement accounts; this is where your allowances and reimbursements are credited to.

4. Fixed deposit account: To park your funds and earn a decent rate of interest on it, there are different types of accounts like fixed deposits and recurring deposits.

A fixed deposit (FD) account allows you to earn a fixed rate of interest for keeping a certain sum of money locked in for a given time, that is until the FD matures. FDs range between a maturity period of seven days to 10 years. The rate of interest you earn on FDs will vary depending on the tenure of the FD. Generally, you cannot withdraw money from an FD before it matures. Some banks offer a premature withdrawal facility. But in that case, the interest rate you earn is lower.

5. Recurring deposit account
A recurring deposit (RD) has a fixed tenure. You need to invest a fixed sum of money in it regularly -- every month or once a quarter -- to earn interest. Unlike FDs, where you need to make a lump sum deposit, the sum you need to invest here is smaller and more frequent. You cannot change the tenure of the RD and the amount to be invested each month or quarter. Even in the case of RDs, you face a penalty in the form of a lower interest rate for premature withdrawal. The maturity period of an RD could range between six months to 10 years.

6. NRI accounts
There are different types of bank accounts for Indians or Indian-origin people living overseas. These accounts are called overseas accounts. They include two types of savings accounts and fixed deposits -- NRO or non-resident ordinary and NRE or non-resident external accounts. Banks also offer foreign currency non-resident fixed deposit accounts. Let us quickly see the various types of bank accounts for NRIs-

a) Non-resident ordinary (NRO) savings accounts or fixed deposit accounts: NRO accounts are rupee accounts. When NRIs deposit money in these accounts, usually in foreign currency, it is converted into INR at the prevailing exchange rate. NRIs can park money earned in India or overseas in NRO bank accounts. Payments like rent, maturities, pension, among others, can be sent abroad through NRO accounts. The income earned on these deposit accounts is taxed.

b) Non-resident external (NRE) savings accounts or fixed deposit accounts: NRE deposit accounts are similar to NRO accounts and the funds in these accounts are maintained in INR. Any money deposited into these accounts is converted into INR at prevailing exchange rates. But, these accounts are only for parking your earnings from abroad. The funds, both principal and interest, are transferable. But, the interest earned on these deposit accounts is not taxed in India.

b) Foreign currency non-resident (FCNR) account: As the name suggests and unlike the other two types of bank accounts, FCNR accounts are maintained in foreign currency. The principal and interest from these accounts are transferable, but the interest earned is not taxed in India.

2. Advancing Loans:

A loan is a credit that you have borrowed from the NBFC or bank with a promise of returning it within a specific period. The lender decides on a fixed rate of interest, which you have to pay along with the principal amount within a specific period. Here are different types of loans available in India. Loans are classified into two factors based on the purpose that they are used for:
Secured loans
Unsecured loans

Secured loans: Secured loans are the ones that require collateral where you have to pledge an asset as security while borrowing from the lender. That way, if you cannot repay the loan, the lender still has some means to get back their money. The rate of interest on secured loans tends to be lower as compared to those for loans without collateral.

What are the types of secured loans?
1. Home loan
Home loans are a secured mode of finance that gives you the funds to buy or build the home of your choice. You can apply online for a home loan at lower interest rates at Bajaj Finance. The following are the types of home loans available in India:

Land purchase loan: To purchase land for your new home
Home construction loan: To build a new home
Home loan balance transfer: Transfer the balance of your existing home loan at a lower interest rate
Top up loan: Can be used to renovate an existing home or have the latest interiors for your new home
Note that while buying a new property/ home, the lender requires you to make a down payment of at least 10-20% of the property's value. The rest is financed. The loan amount disbursed depends on your income, its stability, and current liabilities, among others.

2. Loan against property (LAP)
A loan against property is one of the most common forms of a secured loan. You can pledge any residential, commercial, or industrial property to avail of the funds required. The loan amount disbursed is equivalent to a certain percentage of the property's value and varies across lenders.
While some lenders may offer an amount equivalent to 50-60% of the property's value, others may offer an amount close to 80%. A loan against property helps you unlock the dormant value of your asset and can be used to satiate personal life goals such as higher education for children or marriage. Businesses use a loan against property for business expansion, R&D and product development, among others.

3. Loans against insurance policies
Yes, you can also avail of loans against your insurance policy. However, note that all insurance policies do not qualify for this. Only policies, such as endowment and money-back policies, which have a maturity value, can avail of loans.
Thus, you cannot avail of a loan against a term insurance plan as it does not have any maturity benefits. Also, loans cannot be availed against unit-linked plans as the returns are not fixed and depend on the market's performance. It is essential to note that you can opt for a loan against endowment and money-back policies only after they have acquired a surrender value. These policies gain a surrender value only after paying regular premiums continuously for three years.

4. Gold loans
For the longest time, gold has been one of the most favored asset classes. The organised Indian gold loan industry is expected to touch Rs. 3,101 billion by 2019-20, according to a KPMG report, thanks to flexible interest rates offered by financial institutions. A gold loan requires you to pledge gold jewellery or coins as collateral. The loan amount sanctioned is a certain percentage of the gold's value pledged. Gold loans are generally used for short-term needs and have a short repayment tenure compared to home loans and loans against property.

5. Loans against mutual funds and shares
Mutual funds can also be pledged as collateral for a loan, an ideal vehicle for long-term wealth creation. You can pledge equity or hybrid funds to the financial institution for availing of a loan. For doing so, you need to write to your financier and execute a loan agreement.
Your financier then will write to the mutual fund registrar and put a lien on the specific number of units to be pledged. Typically, you can get 60-70% of the value of units pledged as a loan.

Similarly, financial institutions create a lien against shares for which the loan is taken, and the loan value is equivalent to a percentage of the value of the shares.

6. Loans against fixed deposits

A fixed deposit not only offers assured returns but can also come in handy when you need a loan. The loan amount can vary between 70-90% of the FD's value and varies across lenders. However, it is essential to note that the loan tenure cannot be more than the FD's tenure.

Unsecured loans

These are loans that do not require collateral. The lender gives you the money based on past associations, your credit score and history. Thus, you have to have a good credit history to avail of these loans. Unsecured loans usually come at a higher interest rate due to the lack of collateral.

What are the types of unsecured loan?

1. Personal loan

A personal loan is one of the most popular types of unsecured loans that offer instant liquidity. However, since a personal loan is an unsecured mode of finance, the interest rates are higher than secured loans. A good credit score and high and stable income ensure you can avail of this loan at a competitive interest rate. Personal loans can be used for the following purposes:

Manage all expenses of a family wedding
Pay for a vacation or an international trip
Finance your home renovation project
Fund the cost of your child's higher education
Consolidate all your debts into a single loan
Meet unexpected/ unplanned/ urgent expenses

What type of loan is a personal loan?

A personal loan is an unsecured loan, which means it does not require any security or collateral and can be obtained with minimal paperwork. The money obtained from this loan can be used for any immediate or unexpected purposes. You must pay it back according to the terms set forth by the lender, just like any other loan.

2. Short-term business loans

Another type of unsecured loan, a short-term business loan, can be used to meet various entities' and organisations' expansion and daily expenses.

Working capital loans
Machinery loans and equipment finance
Small business loans for MSMEs
Loans for women entrepreneurs
Loans for traders
Loans for manufacturers
Loans for service enterprises

Which type of loan is the cheapest?

Depending on your credit score, income, and other eligibility requirements, the affordability of a loan may change. Secured loans are typically a more affordable choice as they are backed by collateral and have lower interest rates than unsecured loans. Unsecured loans lack any form of collateral security, which results in higher interest rates. But, the interest rate should not be the sole consideration when applying for a personal loan. The loan approval process, documentation, stamp duty, and other factors should also be considered while applying for a loan.

What are Flexi Loans?

With a Flexi loan, you can avail of funds from your approved limit and, withdraw the amount whenever required and pay interest only on the amount you have utilised. You can withdraw on your loan limit any number of times and prepay when you have extra cash at no additional cost. Such a unique facility gives you the freedom to fully control your finances, unlike Term Loans, Flexi Personal Loans offer you savings on your EMIs by up to 45%. Here, you also have the option to pay only interest as EMIs, with the principal payable at the end of the tenure.

CHEQUES - TYPES AND CROSSING OF CHEQUES

Section 6 of the Negotiable Instrument Act defines a cheque as, "A bill of exchange drawn on a specified banker and not expressed to be payable otherwise than on demand.

In simple words: A cheque is a kind of bill of exchange or an unconditional order in writing, addressed by a customer with signature to the bank to pay a certain amount to the bearer or as per order.

Bills of Exchange - It is a written and signed order directing the person named in it to pay a certain amount of money only to, or to the order of a certain person or to the bearer.

Parties of Cheques:

DRAWER - The person who signs the cheque and order for payment.

DRAWEE - It is always bank on which cheque is drawn and is ordered to pay the amount of cheque

PAYEE - The person to whom the cheque is payable. (In many cases, drawer and payee can be the same person.)

Types of Cheques:

(A) OPEN CHEQUE - It is an uncrossed cheque which is payable at the counter of the bank. It can be Bearer Cheque or Order Cheque

(B) BEARER CHEQUE - When a cheque is payable to a person whose name appears on the cheque or to the bearer i.e. to the person who presents the cheque to the bank for encashment, it is called bearer cheque. It can be transferred by mere delivery and does not need endorsement.

(C) ORDER CHEQUE - When a cheque is payable to a person named in the cheque or to his order, it is called Order Cheque. When the word Bearer is canceled, the cheque becomes the order cheque. It can be transferred only by endorsement and delivery.

(D) CROSSED CHEQUE - It is the cheque on which two parallel transverse lines are drawn across the top left, with or without the word
(i) '& Co.'
(in) Not Negotiable
(in) A/c Payee
It can not be encashed at the counter of the bank, can only be credited to the account of the payee

(E) STALE CHEQUE - The validity of cheque is for three months. It cheque is not presented within the three months, it got expired and becomes the Stale Cheque or Out-dated cheque. Earlier the validity of cheque was for six months, it has been reduced to three months, with effect from April 1, 2012.

(F) ANTE- DATED CHEQUE - A cheque contains the date on which it is drawn. If it bears a prior date or back date, it is called Ante-Dated cheque. Bank will honour this cheque until it exceed the three months, i.e. stale period of cheque.

(G) POST-DATED CHEQUE - If the cheque bears the date later than the date on which it is drawn, is called Post-Dated Cheque. This cheque can not be honoured before the date written on it.

(H) MULTILATED CHEQUE - A cheque which is torn into pieces is called Multilated cheque.

Crossing of Cheques: Crossing of Cheques means to draw two lines transverse parallel on the left hand corner of the cheque. It directs the bank to deposit the money directly into the account and not to pay cash at the bank counter.

MODES OF CROSSING: Below are the modes of crossing of cheques and the effect of crossing of cheques:

1 GENERAL CROSSING - When a cheque bears two transverse parallel lines at the left hand of its top corner. Words such as 'and company' or any other abbreviation (such as & co.) may be written between these two parallel lines, either with or without words 'not negotiable', is called General Crossing.

Effect - Payment can be paid through bank account only and should not be made at the counter of the paying bank.

(2) SPECIAL CROSSING - When a cheque bears the name of the bank in between the two parallel lines, with or without the words 'not negotiable' is called Special Crossing.

Effect - The bank will pay to the banker whose name is written in between the crossing lines.

(3) RESTRICTIVE CROSSING /ACCOUNT PAYEE CROSSING - In this, crossing of cheques is done by writing Account Payee or Account Payee only in between the crossing lines.

Effect - Payment will be credited to the account of payee named in the cheque.

(4) DOUBLE CROSSING - When a cheque bears two special crossing, is called Double Crossing. In this second bank act as agent of the first collecting banker. It is made when the banker in whose favour the cheque is crossed does not have branch where the cheque is paid.

AUTOMATED TELLER MACHINE (ATM)

Everything About Automated Teller Machine (ATM)

1.What is the Full form of an ATM?
Ans: Automated Teller Machine

2. How much does the bank charge when you check your account balance on an ATM after the free Transaction limit?
Ans: 5 Rs per enquiry.

3. How much does the Bank charge beyond the Transaction limit?
Ans: Rs 20 per transaction.

4. What is the time Limit for resolving customer's complaint related to ATMs by issuing Banks?
Ans: Within 7 Working Days from the date of receipt of customer complaint.

5. In case failure to re-credit a customer's account within 7 Days how much compensation is paid to the customer by the bank?
Ans: Rs 100 per day

6. In case the compensation is not credited as mandated, what recourse does the customer have?
Ans: For all such complaints customers may lodge a complaint with the local Banking Ombudsman if the bank does not respond.

7. Name the first Bank to introduce an ATM in India?
Ans: Hongkong and Shanghai Banking Corporation (HSBC)

8. Name the first Bank to provide Mobile ATM service in India?
Ans: ICICI bank

9. India's First Talking ATM has been launched by which Bank?
Ans: Union Bank of India

10. Non-Bank owned ATM are also known as ____ .
Ans: White Label ATMs

11. Name India's First Company to open White Label ATMs?
Ans: Tata Communications Payments Solutions Ltd
The first company to get RBI's permission to open White Label ATMs is Tata Communications Payment Solutions Limited (TCPSL). TCPSL started their White Label ATMs chain under the brand name "Indicash".

12. India's First Non-Bank owned ATM (White Label ATMs) opened in which State?
Ans: Maharashtra (in Thane District)

13. Which city got the country's first Talking ATM?
Ans: Ahmedabad, Gujarat

14. Talking ATM has what kind of Special Interface?
Ans: Voice Interface

15. Who inaugurated the country's first Talking ATM?
Ans: Chairman and Managing Director of Union Bank of India, D Sarkar.

16. Which was the second bank to launch a Talking ATM in India?
Ans: State Bank of India

17. What are the types of cards that can be used at an ATM?
Ans: The ATM cards/debit cards, credit cards and prepaid cards (that permit cash withdrawal)

18. Who was the Inventor of ATM?
Ans: John Adrian Shepherd Barron (A Britisher)

19. Inventor John Shepherd Barron installed the world's first automatic cash dispenser at which place in the world?
Ans: Barclays Bank Branch, near London

20. ATM machine was invented in the year _____:
Ans: 1967

21. The first Machine was called by the name of.
Ans: De La Rue Automatic Cash System (DACS)

22. India's Highest and World's second Highest ATM is located at:
Ans: Sikkim
On 12 December 2003 UTI Bank inaugurated its ATM at Thegu, Near the Nathu - La pass in Sikkim. The Height of the ATM is near about 13,200 Feet above the sea level. The ATM is opened there for the convenience of Indian Army Personnel of that area. On Dec 12, 2003 UTI Bank inaugurated an ATM at Thegu, Near Bathu-La pass Sikkim.

23. The World's Highest ATM is located at?
Ans: Pakistan by the Pakistan National Bank in 2016.

24. White Label ATM means:
Ans: The ATM that does not have any bank logo.

Types of ATM:

1. Bank's own ATMs: These ATMs are owned and operated by the owner bank and the machines carry the Bank's logo. Such ATMs are the costliest way of providing ATM services.

2. White Label ATMs (WLAs): These ATMs are owned and operated by a non-banking company but it provides service to the customers of every bank. These ATMs are interconnected with the entire network of ATMs in the country and carry the logo of the company owning them. These ATMs don't work on any banks behalf. They are independent. But they are tied up with a sponsor bank just only to provide the cash.

3. Brown Label ATMs (BLAs): These ATMs are owned and operated by third parties (non-banking companies). The operating cost from rent, electricity to everything is borne by the company. But the ATMs carry the logo of the bank outsourcing the service.

The concerned bank only handles a part of the process which involves back-end server connectivity and handling cash. This business is between the ATM services company and the bank. The bank asked the ATM service company to work on their behalf.

4. On-site ATM: When the branch and ATM are in the same premises then it is called On-site ATM.

5. Off-site ATM: When the branch and ATM is located in different place but on the same town or city then it is called off-site ATM.

6. Green label ATMs are used for Agricultural transactions.

7. Orange label ATM is used for transacting shares.

8. Yellow label ATMs are used for E-commerce.

9. Pink label ATMs are used for women's banking.

Types of Transactions in ATM:

On-U's transactions: When we withdraw cash from the ATM of a bank where we don't have our account (savings/current) then it is called On-U's.

Off-U's transactions: When we withdraw cash from the ATM of a bank where we have our account (savings/current) then it is called Off-U's.

Some MCQs on ATM:

A. Which among the following is correct about the "White Label ATM":
a) Any non-bank entity with a minimum net worth of Rs. 100 crores can apply for white label ATMs. (Not Just NBFCs, any non-bank entity can apply)
b) White Label ATMs do not carry any bank logo.
c) RBI has given license/permission to non-bank entities to open White Label ATMs.
d) Sponsor Bank provides the cash.
e) None of These

f) All of the Above (correct)

B. Which among the following is correct about Brown Label ATMs?
a) These ATMs are owned and maintained by service providers.
b) Bank whose Brand name is used on the ATM takes care of cash management and network connectivity.
c) Both of Above (correct)
d) None of These

C. Which among the following definitions are correct.
a) Online ATMS - These ATMs are connected to the bank's database at all times and provide real time transactions online. The withdrawal limits and account balances are constantly monitored by the bank.
b) Offline ATMs - These ATMs are not connected to the bank's database hence they have a predefined withdrawal limit fixed and you can withdraw that amount irrespective of the balance in your account.
c) Both of the Above (correct)
d) None of These

D. Which among the following definitions of ATMs are incorrect?
a) Onsite ATM - The ATMs are installed within a branch premises.
b) Stand Alone ATM - The ATMs are not connected with any ATM network hence their transactions are restricted to the ATM's branch and link branches only.
c) Both of Above
d) None of These (correct)

E. ATMs cards are issued to a person who maintains which of the following accounts with the bank?
1. saving bank accounts
2. Current accounts
3. term deposits
4. either 1 or 2 (correct)

F. Biometric ATM cards are generally issued for which of the following?

1. Illiterates
2. Sick & old persons
3. Inoperative account holders
4. Both 1 & 2 (correct)

G. Which of the following is also known as a Bank owned ATM?
1. White label ATM
2. Brown label ATM
3. Green label ATM
4. On site ATM (correct)

H. What does O stand for in WLAO?
A) Organiser
B) Operator (correct)
C) Ordinary
D) Ordinance
White Label ATM Operator (WLAO)

The 21st century banking or next generation banking is all about the internet, Artificial Intelligence (AI) and Machine Learning (ML). This is also known as the New Age Banking or New Era of banking.

The new age banking products and technologies in India are a gift by the National Payments Corporation of India (NPCI), which is a specialized division of the Reserve Bank of India under the jurisdiction of the Ministry of Finance, Government of India.

1. What is National Payments Corporation of India (NPCI)?

Ans: NPCI is a not-for-profit organization registered under Section 8 of the Companies Act 2013, established by the Reserve Bank of India and Indian Banks' Association. It was Founded in 19 December 2016 and was Headquartered in Mumbai, Maharashtra, India.

The organization is owned by a consortium of major banks and has been promoted by the country's central bank, the Reserve Bank of India. Simply the Owner is Reserve Bank of India, Ministry of Finance, Government of India. The Website is: www.npci.org.in. It was created by the RBI for operating retail payments and settlement systems in India.

The Products of NPCI are:
a. Aadhaar Enabled Payment System
b. Bharat Bill Payment System
c. BHIM
d. Cheque Truncation System
e. Immediate Payment Service
f. National Automated Clearing House
g. National Common Mobility Card
h. National Financial Switch
i. NUUP Services
j. Query Service on Aadhaar Mapper (*99*99#)
k. RuPay
l. Unified Payments Interface

2. What is the international wing of the NPCI?

Ans: NPCI International Payments Limited (NIPL). NPCI has created a separate subsidiary to take its product to the global market. The organization is getting offers from nations around Asia, Africa and the Middle East to improve their payment infrastructure. Internationalization of RuPay and Unified Payment Interface (UPI) are the primary focus of the NPCI International Payments Limited (NIPL).

3. What is the new subsidiary company of the Bharat Bill Payment System (BBPS) created by NPCI?

Ans: NPCI Bharat BillPay Limited (NBBL). In April 2021, NPCI created a new subsidiary for Bharat Bill Payment System (BBPS) to increase growth especially in the business to consumer segment for small businesses. This is done in view of growing traffic and workload from UPI, IMPS, Aadhaar Enabled Payment System and National Electronic Toll Collections. NBBL is a public company registered in December 2020

Aadhaar Enabled Payment System: A network of Micro ATMs using Aadhaar authentication. National Payments Corporation of India (NPCI) announced the transactions of Aadhaar Enabled Payment System (AePS) for the month of July 2019 have crossed the milestone number of 200 million. AePS is a bank-led model which allows basic interoperable banking transactions at PoS (Micro ATM) through the Business correspondent of any bank by using Aadhaar authentication.

Bharat Bill Payment System (BBPS): The Bharat Bill Payment System is a Reserve Bank of India (RBI) conceptualized system driven by the NPCI. It is a one-stop ecosystem for payment of all bills, providing an interoperable and accessible "Anytime Anywhere" bill payment service to all customers across India with certainty, reliability and safety. Bharat BillPay has multiple modes of payment and provides instant confirmation of payment via an SMS or receipt. It offers myriad bill collection categories like electricity, telecom, DTH, gas, water bills etc. through a single window. More categories may be added in the future, to include insurance premium, mutual funds, school fees, institution fees, credit cards, local taxes, invoice payments, etc. An effective mechanism for handling consumer complaints has also been put in place. Bharat BillPay transactions can be initiated through multiple payment channels like Internet, Internet Banking, Mobile, Mobile-Banking, POS (Point of Sale terminal), Mobile Wallets, MPOS (Mobile Point of Sale terminal), Kiosk, ATM, Bank Branch, Agents and Business Correspondents. Bharat BillPay supports multiple payment modes. This includes Cards (Credit, Debit and Prepaid), NEFT Internet Banking, UPI, Wallets, Aadhaar based Payments and Cash.

BharatQR: A common QR code developed by NPCI in collaboration with American Express, Mastercard and Visa for ease of payments and interoperability.

BHIM: BHIM is a mobile app to act as Client software for the Unified Payments Interface.

BHIM Aadhaar Pay: BHIM Aadhaar pay is an Aadhaar based payments interface which allows real time payments to Merchants using the Aadhaar number of Customers & authenticating them through their biometrics.

Cheque Truncation System (CTS): CTS is based on a cheque truncation or online image-based cheque clearing system where cheque images and magnetic ink character recognition (MICR) data are captured at the collecting bank branch and transmitted electronically.

Immediate Payment Service (IMPS): Immediate Payment Service is a real time interbank payment system.

Mobile number & MMID: Send money to bank accounts mapped using mobile number. Account number & IFSC: Send money to bank accounts.

National Automated Clearing House: A centralized clearing service that aims at providing interbank high volume, low value transactions that are repetitive and periodic in nature.

National Common Mobility Card - Rupay Contactless
Rupay Contactless is a contactless payment technology that allows cardholders to wave their card in front of contactless payment terminals without the need to physically swipe or insert the card into a point-of-sale device.

National Electronic Toll Collection
FASTag is a device that employs Radio Frequency Identification (RFID) technology for making toll payments directly while the vehicle is in motion. FASTag (RFID Tag) is affixed on the windscreen of the vehicle and enables a customer to make the toll payments directly from the account which is linked to FASTag. The latest version 2.0 can also be used to buy fuel. IDFC First Bank has become the first one to get an approval from the RBI. The Ministry of Road Transport and Highways (MoRTH) has declared that all lanes at all toll plazas on national highways across the country will be dedicated Fastag lanes from 1, December 2019.

National Financial Switch: Network of shared automated teller machines in India.

RuPay: RuPay is a domestic card scheme of India. The card has Magnetic stripe (for Backward compatibility) and an EMV chip. The RuPay card is now accepted at all ATMs, Point-of-Sale terminals and most online merchants in the country. More than 300 cooperative banks and Regional Rural Banks (RRBs) in the country have also issued RuPay ATM cards.

Unified Payments Interface (UPI): The Owner of UPI is the National Payments Corporation of India. It was Introduced in 11 April 2016. Unified Payments Interface is a real-time interbank payment system for sending or receiving money. It is integrated with more than 120 banks in India. Consumers can participate in P2P transfer as long as they both have an account in one of the registered banks. To initiate fund transfer, users have to use any UPI supporting Android or iOS app, link their bank accounts and generate BHIM UPI PIN. Funds can be transferred via the following methods:

Virtual Payment Address (VPA): Send or request money from/to bank account mapped using VPA.
Account number & IFSC: Send money to bank account.
QR code: Send money by scanning QR code with enclosed VPA or Account number & IFSC.
Mobile number: Send or request money from/to the bank account mapped using mobile number.
Aadhaar: Send money to the bank account mapped using Aadhaar number.
Once the fund transfer is initiated, money is debited from the payer's bank account and deposited in the recipient's bank account in real-time. This system works 24x7, including weekends and bank holidays.

***99# USSD:** An USSD channel service for UPI mobile banking launched in November 2012. Only public sector telecom service providers Bharat Sanchar Nigam Limited BSNL and Mahanagar Telephone Nigam Limited MTNL are offering this service. It uses quick codes for transactions and doesn't require a smartphone and access to the internet. The interface is developed by National Unified USSD Platform (NUUP) to overcome the problem of poor internet connectivity in rural areas with 12 regional languages. This service is currently offered by 51 banks. BHIM app also supports USSD features. Understanding the importance of mobile banking in financial inclusion in general and of *99# in particular, various regulatory/trade bodies came together to ensure on boarding of all TSPs on *99# (USSD 1.0). With the wider ecosystem (11 TSPs), *99# was launched by Prime minister Narendra Modi on 28 August 2014, as part of Pradhan Mantri Jan Dhan Yojna.

UPI Pay123: It is a 3-step method to initiate and execute UPI services for feature phone users without the use of internet connection or USSD channel. It is based on Interactive voice response (IVR) technology which is good especially for rural areas. It is launched by RBI on 10 March 2022.

Digi Saathi: It is a 24x7 helpline for digital payments. It was launched with UPI Pay123 by the RBI on 10 March 2022.

Kiosk:
What Is Kiosk Banking? Eligibility, Benefits and Purpose

Banking and its ancillary activities have been an integral component of one's daily routine. The banks handle all from monitoring balances to cashing cheques. Banking companies have also chosen technologies like ATMs in this era of inventing solutions that simplify human life. The availability of ATMs has streamlined procedures such as the transfer of funds and money withdrawal. Because of this, it has received acceptance among ordinary working people who can obtain cash quickly and easily. However, these resources have long been out of range for the poor and minorities of the community. This sector primarily consists of daily wage workers who cannot access banking institutes for basic services. By establishing the well-known kiosk banking method, the RBI successfully closed this gap.

The Full Form of KIOSK is Kommunikasjon Integrert Offentlig Service Kontor.

What Are Some Kiosk Types?
There are mainly 5 types of Kiosks. They are:

Information Kiosk: An information kiosk is a non-interactive or interactive kiosk that displays information or gives it through a menu system. The information kiosks offered at your local library, for example, provide an active catalogue of their holdings. Another example would be the kiosks found in malls and stores that exhibit popular items in their inventory.

Interactive Kiosk: Customers can interact with interactive kiosks, which are not static. Retailers, restaurants, service firms, and tourist locations such as malls and airports all use interactive kiosks. Customers can use interactive kiosks for directions and navigation, self-service ordering or check-in, making purchases, or even getting online.

Wayfinding Kiosk: A wayfinding kiosk's goal is to assist users in determining where they are and how to get to their target location. This might be accomplished by displaying a simple 2D map with the current location highlighted. Different floors are represented by different colors in this modeling approach.

Temperature Kiosk: A temperature kiosk uses an infrared camera to scan the user and record their temperature. The kiosk will notify the user if the temperature is too high. Some temperature scanners can be linked to door access, allowing you to refuse entry to anyone who registers a high temperature. Temperature screening, according to the WHO, should be included in a package of COVID-19 prevention and control measures in the workplace. Preventing possibly sick individuals from entering your workplace gives an extra layer of disease protection. It might also help reassure your employees that they are returning to a safe working environment.

Internet Kiosk: These kiosks, which are commonly located in public waiting areas or hotel reception areas, allow users to access the internet. The user will be able to browse the web for a price at one of these terminals for a certain period of time. After that period has passed, the system will lock, and the user will have to pay an extra price to gain access again. These types of kiosks are vulnerable to cyber-attacks and hackers because they are connected to the internet. It's critical to make sure your internet kiosks are protected with antispyware and antivirus software. Any attempts to hijack your system or steal confidential user information will be detected by these.

Self-Service Kiosks: A self-service kiosk is a device that allows customers to engage with businesses without having to wait for a staff. They can be used in a variety of situations, but frequent examples include purchasing rail tickets or dining at restaurants with a quick payment system. The goal is to reduce line sizes and speed up the payment procedure.

Kiosk Banking and Its Meaning: KIOSK is an acronym for Kommunikasjon Integrert Offentlig Service Kontor, and it refers to a compact open-fronted tent or booth. In regard to the bank, the design of the kiosk facility is to meet the financial requirement of low-income individuals by providing conventional financial services closer to their homes. People can use the kiosk to obtain banking services like cheque transfers, money transfers, balance inquiries, cash deposits, and remittances. One can do all these activities without visiting the bank. The low-income groups gain from this since they obtain all of the facilities without going to the banks. Because these people are incompetent at keeping a minimum balance in respective savings accounts, the kiosk allows people to do so without worry.

The two important parts of the kiosk financial system are:
Customer Service Point (CSP)
Kiosk machine

Customer Service Point: This is a desk in the business that works in tandem with the kiosk cubicle to provide quick access to private or government banks. Users can access the Customer Service Point with any questions or concerns about payments or accounts operations, and the Customer Service Point will respond.

Kiosk Machine: The kiosk machines are the second part of the kiosk booths, and it enables users to make transactions and certain other activities like cheque deposits, status queries, etc. This machine has the below parts in it.
Barcode scanner
Touch and non-touch display
Money acceptor
Incorporated a full-page thermal copier
Incorporated speakers
Keyboard along with the trackball
Video camera

Who Can Start a Kiosk Banking System?
Shop keepers, merchants, micro-enterprises and perhaps even individuals are eligible to apply to start a kiosk system. The following are the requirements for kiosk banking:
The age requirement is 18 years old.
Academic Credentials: The applicant must have a senior secondary school assessment pass certificate.
The kiosk cubicle requires at least 100-200 square feet for establishment.
The candidate must guarantee that PCs and internet access are available.
Store owners or micro-enterprises can combine a kiosk stall with a Customer Service Point, but the small company must have to register as an MSME. The financial institution must provide the necessary tools for constructing a kiosk, which contains a kiosk device, a device for inspecting fingerprints and applications interoperable with desktops.

Kiosk vs ATM
After the invention of the ATM, there was establishment of kiosk financing institutions. As a consequence, there are certain distinctions between the kiosk and ATMs, and we can explain them by the facilities supplied by kiosks, which include: Account inquiries, like cheque book demands, are available at kiosks, which aren't available at ATMs.
Users can also use kiosks to access client support technologies that directly contact the institution's support centre.
ATMs do not give MIS monitoring, whereas kiosks do.
A further notable distinction between a kiosk and an Automated Teller Machine is that a kiosk enables the depositing of cheques.
Digital banking is also available at kiosks, allowing users to make online payments.
A CSP is also available at kiosks to help people.

What is Kiosk Banking?
Today, banking kiosks - broadly known as ATMs (automated teller machines) - are available at a number of different locations. As some of the first kiosks in common use, they have been popular for decades and have come to be trusted by the vast majority of consumers. Today we will discuss the reasons why banking kiosks have maintained their place at the top for so many years.

What is kiosk banking and what are the benefits?
Kiosk banking allows users to access traditional banking functions such as deposits and withdrawals, as well as transfer money between accounts and check their balances, all from the convenience of a kiosk. The primary purpose of kiosk banking is to provide easy access and accessibility to as many people as possible, regardless of the time of day.

Chatbot:

What is a chatbot?
Chatbot is a software or computer program that simulates human conversation or "chatter" through text or voice interactions.

Users in both business-to-consumer (B2C) and business-to-business (B2B) environments increasingly use chatbot virtual assistants to handle simple tasks. Adding chatbot assistants reduces overhead costs, uses support staff time better and enables organizations to provide customer service during hours when live agents aren't available.

A chatbot is an artificial intelligence (AI) program that can simulate a conversation (or a chat) with a user in natural language through messaging applications, websites, mobile applications or by phone.

INTERNATIONAL BANKING

What is International Banking?
Ans: International banking is a type of banking which has branches across the national border. It is the same as the national bank but it also provides the same service to the international clients also. It covers both the type of clients like individuals and businesses.

What are the types of services that were offered in international banking?
Ans: Services are:
1) To arrange trade finance an international bank arranges the finance for the traders who want to deal with the foreign country.
2) To arrange foreign exchange the core services provided by the international bank are to arrange a foreign exchange for the import-export purpose.
3) To hedge the funds the international bank hedge the funds by buying the securities at the lower price level and sell it when the
price level rising.
4) Offer investment banking services it also offers an investment banking services by signing underwriting of shares, financial decisions for investment.

What are the types of International banking:

1) Correspondent banks
Correspondent banks involve the relationship between different banks which are in different countries. This type of bank is generally used by the multinational companies for their international banking. This type of banks is small in size and provides service to those clients who are out of their country.

2) Edge act banks
Edge act banks are based on the constitutional amendment of 1919. They will operate business internationally under the amendment.

3) Off-shore banking centre

It is a type of banking sector which allows foreign accounts. Offshore banking is free from the banking regulation of that particular country. It provides all types of products and services.

4) Subsidiaries

Subsidiaries are the banks which incorporate in one country which is either partially or completely owned by "parent bank in another country. The affiliates are somewhat different from the subsidiaries like it is not ruined by a parent bank and it works independently.

5) Foreign branch bank

Foreign banks are the banks which are legally tied up with the parent bank but operate in a foreign nation. A foreign bank follows the rules and regulations of both the countries i.e. home country and a host country.

Name the types of risks involved in international banking?
Ans: Risks are:

1) Currency risk

An international bank has to be familiar with the currency exchange rate while doing business internationally. The companies which choose to operate in a foreign country and at that time it has to deal with currency risk.

2) Political risk

Political risk also affects the business because business has to follow the rules and regulation of host country and each country has their political effect on the business. If the political decisions are unfavorable it affects the business.

3) Reputation risk

A reputation risk means the potential loss in reputational capital based on either real or observed loss in reputational capital. A bank faces reputation risks like rumours about the bank, data manipulation, bad customer service, and experience. A bank's reputation is judged by the clients, investors, leaders, and critics.

4) Systematic risk

The systematic risk is not related to a particular bank but it affects the whole economy. A systematic risk is associated with failures of the big entity and it affects the whole economy.

Examples of international banking:
City group
HSBC Holdings
Bank of America
JP Morgan Chase
Royal Bank of Scotland Group.

Foreign exchange reserves: Components of Forex total Reserves
1.1 Foreign Currency Assets
1.2 Gold
1.3 SDRS
1.4 Reserve Position in the IMF

Reserves are maintained by countries for meeting their international payment obligations both short and long terms, including sovereign and commercial debts, financing of imports,
for intervention in the foreign currency markets during periods of volatility, besides helping to boost the confidence of the market in the ability of a country to meet its external obligations and to absorb any unforeseen external shocks, contingencies or unexpected capital movements.

India's foreign exchange reserves comprise foreign currency assets, gold and special drawing rights allocated to it by the International Monetary Fund (IMF) in addition to the reserves it has parked with the fund. Foreign exchange reserves are held and managed by
the RBI.

The Foreign currency assets are investment mainly in instruments abroad which have the highest credit rating and which do not pose any credit risk. These include sovereign bonds, treasury bills and short-term deposits in top-rated global banks besides cash accounts.

The Special Drawing Right (SDR) is an interest-bearing international reserve asset created by the IMF in 1969 to supplement other reserve assets of member countries. The SDR is based on a basket of international currencies comprising the U.S. dollar, Japanese
yen, euro and pound sterling. It is not a currency, nor a claim on the IMF, but is potentially a claim on freely usable currencies of IMF members. It can be held and used by member countries, the IMF, and certain designated official entities called "prescribed holders."-but it can not be held, for example, by private entities or individuals.

Bank for International Settlements: Banker To All Central Banks
The Bank for International Settlements (BIS) is an international organization which was formed in 1930 with the objective of serving the Central Banks of various nations, aiding them to develop an environment of monetary and financial stability via concerted efforts to bring about International co-operation.
The Bank for International Settlements popularly termed as "Bank for Central Banks" has its headquarters in Basel, Switzerland, came into being consequent of the provisions of Hague Agreement of 1930.

CAMELS Rating System:

CAMELS is a rating system developed in the US that is used by supervisory authorities to rate banks and other financial institutions. It applies to every bank in the U.S and is also used by various financial institutions outside the U.S. This rating system was adopted by the National Credit Union Administration in 1987. In 1988, the Basel Committee on Banking Supervision of the Bank of International Settlements

(BIS) proposed the CAMELS framework for assessing financial institutions.

Camels composite rating:
The CAMELS system is also based on composite ratings on a scale of one to five based on ascending order of supervisory concern. Each factor is assigned a weight as follows:

Capital adequacy 20 %
Asset quality 20%
Management 25%
Earnings 15%
Liquidity 10%
Sensitivity 10%

The six factors are represented by the acronym "CAMELS."
C- Capital adequacy
A - Asset quality
M - Management quality
E- Earnings
L- Liquidity
S- Sensitivity to Market Risk

FERA and FEMA

In 1973, the Foreign Exchange Regulation Act or FERA was passed in India which brought strict regulations on payments and receivables in the forex and securities department and the import and export of currency.
In 1999, the Foreign Exchange Management Act or FEMA was passed in 1999 in India. It sought "to consolidate and amend the law relating to foreign exchange to facilitate external trade and payments and promote the orderly development and maintenance of foreign exchange market in India."

1. FERA, or the Foreign Exchange Regulation Act, was passed in 1973 by the Parliament of India. FEMA, or the Foreign Exchange Management Act, was passed on December 29, 1999, by the Parliament. FEMA replaced FERA.

2. It was on January 1, 1974, that FERA came into force. In June 2000, FEMA replaced FERA.

3. The Vajpayee government of 1998 repealed FERA. FEMA was enacted to replace FERA.

Foreign Accounts: Nostro, Vostro and Loro Accounts.

Here we will discuss the foreign bank accounts of Indian banks.

Q. What is a Nostro Account?

Ans: When an Indian Bank Opens an account in any branch of a foreign bank in foreign country and currency then that account is a nostro account for the Indian bank in order to provide customer service in that respective abroad country.

```
India.            Usa
SBI. ————————>. BOA
     Opens ac in $
```

This account opened by SBI in BOA's any branch in the USA than that account is a Nostro Account for an Indian Bank SBI to provide customer service abroad. (In terms of Indian bank SBI's perspective)

Q. What is a Vostro Account?

Ans: When an Foreign Bank Opens an account in any branch of any Indian bank in India in Rupees then that account is a vostro account for the Indian bank in order to provide customer service for the abroad citizens in India.

```
India.            Usa
SBI. <————————. BOA
     Opens ac in ₹
```

This account is a vostro account in terms of Indian bank SBI's perspective.

Q. What is a Loro Account?

Ans: When a different Indian bank uses the Noro Account of any other Indian bank then it becomes a Loro Account for the former bank who uses it.

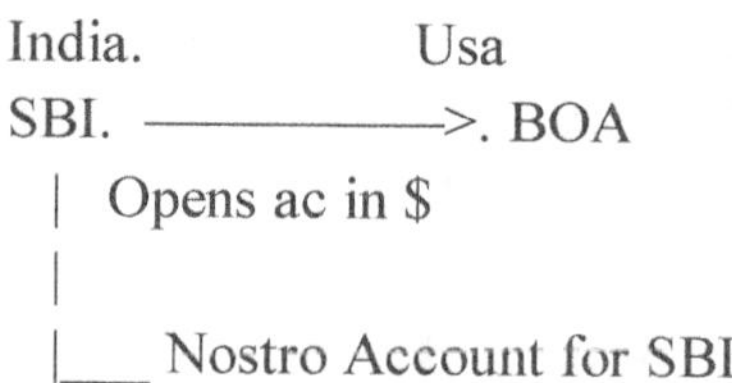

```
India.            Usa
SBI. ————————>. BOA
  | Opens ac in $
  |
  |___ Nostro Account for SBI
```

If PNB uses this nostro account of the SBI then it becomes a LORO account for the PNB.

INTERNATIONAL ORGANIZATION:

World bank:

WB is group of organizations, which include -
International Bank for Reconstruction and Development (IBRD)
International Development Association (DA)
International Finance Corporation (IFC)
Multilateral Investment Guarantee Agency (MIGA)
International Centre for the Settlement of Investment Disputes (ICSID)

Is India a member of all organizations of WB?
Ans: No, India a member of all organizations except ICSID

WB was established in ____.
Ans: Dec. 1945

WB started functioning in ____.
Ans: June 1946.

WB is headquartered at ___.
Ans: Washington DC

WB and IMF are ____ organization.
Ans: complementary

Generally, every member country of the IMF automatically becomes the member of WB. Similarly, any country which quits IMF is automatically expelled from the WB's
membership.

WB was established on the basis of the recommendation of the ____.
Ans: Bretton Wood Conference

WB was established with ____.
Ans: IMF

____ & WB are called Bretton Wood Twins.
Ans: IMF

____ is popularly known as the World Bank.
Ans: IBRD

What are the objectives of WB?
Ans: Providing capital to member countries for economic reconstruction and development. Promoting capital investment in member countries. Increase in productivity of the member countries in order to improve economic conditions and standard of living.

Capital Resources of WR
On June 30, 1996, the authorized capital of the WB was $ 188 billion out of which $ 180.6 billion (96% of total authorized capital) was issued to member countries in the form of shares:
Member countries repay the share amount to the WB in the following ways-
(1) 2% of alloted share are repaid in Gold, US $ or SDR. (2) 18% of its capital share in its own currency. (3) The remaining 80% share deposited by the member country, only on demand by WB

International Bank for Reconstruction and Development (IBRD):

IBRD is popularly known as ____.
Ans: World Bank

IBRD was established on ____.
Ans: Dec 1945

IBRD started functioning on ____.
Ans: June 1946.

What is the primary function of IBRD?
Ans: It aims to reduce poverty in middle-income and creditworthy poorer countries by promoting sustainable development through loans guarantees, risk management products, and analytical and advisory services.

International Development Association (IDA):

IDA is known as _____ of WB.
Ans: Soft loan window

IDA was established on _____
Ans: Sep. 24, 1960

What is the primary function of IDA?
Ans: IDA provides long term interest free loans to its member countries. These loans are provided to the poor countries of the world.

IDAs is administered by _____.
Ans: The same group which manages the working of WB.

International Finance Corporation (IFC):

IFC was established in _____.
Ans: July 1956

What is the primary function of IFC?
Ans: The main work of IFC is to ensure financial support to the private sector in developing countries. It provides loans to private industries of developing nations without any Govt. guarantee.

International Monetary Fund (IMF):

The IMF was established on _____.
Ans: Dec. 7, 1945

IMF was established on Dec. 7, 1945, in _____.
Ans: Washington

IMF was formed on the recommendation of the _____.
Ans: Bretton Woods Conference

IMF started its operation on _____.
Ans: March 1, 1947

How the IMF is being managed and controlled?
Ans: The IMF is controlled and managed by a BOARD OF GOVERNORS. Each member country nominates a Governor. Each Governor is allotted a number of Votes, which is determined by the quota allotted to each country Quota is allotted according to contribution in the IMF Capital.

Each Governor has got the night of 250 votes on the basis of the membership and one additional vote for each SDR 1,00,000 of quota.

That is the reason why the rich and industrialized countries got the higher voting right due to their higher quota, with the IMF. The main source of IMF resources is the quota allotted to member countries. Till 1971, all the amounts of quotas and the assistance provided were denominated in US dollar but since Dec 1971 all the quotas and transaction of IMF are expressed in SDR (Special Drawing Right)

SDR (Special Drawing Right) is also known as _____.
Ans: paper Gold

The IMFs financial year is from _____.
Ans: 1 May to 30 April.

The finance minister is ex-office Governor in IMF Boards of Governors..

World Trade Organization (WTO):

On Oct 30, 1947, 23 countries at Geneva signed an agreement related to tariffs imposed on trade, This agreement is known as General - Agreement on Tariffs and Trade (GATT). It came into force on Jan 1948. On Dec 12, 1995, GATT was abolished and replaced by the World Trade organization (WTO) which came into existence on Jan. 1.4.1995. The Uruguay round of GATT gave birth to world Trade Organization.

WTO's headquarters is in _____.
Ans: Geneva

WTO is not an agency of the _____.
Ans: United Nations organization

WTO has a general Council for its administration, which includes one permanent representative of each member nation. Generally, it has one meeting per month which is held at Geneva. The highest authority of policy making is WTO's ministerial conference which is held after every 2 years. There are a number of important committees for administration of WTO, out of which, 2 committees May the pivotal role in WTO. They are;
(a) Dispute settlement Body - DSB
(b) Trade Policy Review Body- TPRB
(c) DSB considers the complaints of member countries against violation of rules by any member country. This body appoints a group of experts to investigate such complaints. This body meets twice a month for such cases.

Asian Development Bank (ADB):

ADB was established in ____.
Ans: Dec 1966

ADB was established on the recommendations of ____.
Ans: Economic commission for Asia and Far East (ECAFE)

ADB Started its functioning on ___.
Ans: Jan 1, 1967

The Head office of the ADB is located at ____.
Ans: Manila (Philippines).

ADB constituted Asian Development Fund in ___, Which provides loans to Asian countries on concessional interest rates.
Ans: 1974

The Aim of ADB is ____.
Ans: To accelerate economic and social development in Asia and the Pacific region.

The chairmanship is always allotted to a ___ native.

Ans: Japanese

South Asian Association for Regional Co-operation (SAARC):

SAARC headquarters is located at ____.
Ans: Kathmandu (Nepal)

SAARC has a total of __ Members as countries.
Ans: 8 (1. India; 2, Pakistan; 3. Nepal; 4. Bangladesh; 5. Bhutan; 6. Sri Lanka; 7. Maldives; 8. Afghanistan)

SAARC was Established on ____.
Ans: December 7-8, 1985

Association of Southeast Asian Nations (ASEAN):

ASEAN has a total of how many members?
Ans: 10 (Indonesia, Malaysia, Philippines, Singapore, Thailand, Brunei, Vietnam, Laos, Myanmar, Cambodia)

ASEAN is Headquartered at ____.
Ans: Jakarta, Indonesia

What is ASEAN + 3?
Ans: Asean + Japan, China and Korea,

What is Asean + 1?
Ans: Asean + India

What is the primary objective of ASEAN?
Ans: The objective of Asean is to promote economic co-operation in South-East Asia and also to- ensure economic stability in the region.

BRICS:

What is BRICS?
Ans: B- Brazil, R- Russia, I- India, C- China, S- South Africa

The first ever summit was held in ____.
Ans: Russian town Yekaterinburg on June 1 6, 2009.

Asia Pacific Economic Co-operation (APEC):

APEC was founded in ____.
Ans: Nov. 1986.

APEC was institutionalised in ____ after meeting in Bangkok.
Ans: June 1992

APEC has a Secretariat in ____.
Ans: Singapore

Name the former Australian Prime Minister who played important an important role
in the formation of APEC?
Ans: Bob Hawk

Amnesty International (AI):

AI is a worldwide ____ organisation?
Ans: Human-rights

AI founded by whom and when?
Ans: A British lawyer, Peter Benson, in 1961.

AI secretariat is located at ____.
Ans: London

Food and Agriculture Organisation (FAO):

FAO is an associate institution of the ___.
Ans: United Nations

FAO was established in ___.
Ans: 1945 at Quebec

FAO is headquartered at ___.
Ans: Rome, Italy.

The primary function of FAO is ___.
Ans: Bridge the gap between the demand for and supply of agricultural products in the world

Greenpeace (GP):

GP is a ___ organisation?
Ans: International environmental organisation.

GP was founded in ___ in ___.
Ans: Canada in 1971

What is the primary aim of GP?
Ans: The primary aim is to highlight and change harmful industrial policies of the government that threaten the environment or the natural world. It further opposes nuclear weapons, off-shore oil drilling, dumping of radioactive wastes into oceans, wildlife hunting and pollution.

Indian Ocean Rim Association for Regional Co-operation (IOR-ARC)

IOR-ARC was established on __.
Ans: 1997.

IOR-ARC was established at ___.
Ans: Port Louis of Mauritius.

The primary Aim of IOR-ARC was ___.
Ans: Promote economic co-operation among the countries in coastal regions of the Indian Ocean. This association will work as a bridge between 3 continents Asia, Africa and Australia.

International Labour organization (ILO):

ILO is the organization of which international body?
Ans: United Nations

ILO is headquartered at ____.
Ans: Geneva

International organization for Standardization (ISO):

The ISO is a ____ federation of national standards bodies.

Ans: non-governmental

ISO was established in ___ in ____.
Ans: 1947 and Geneva.

What is the primary function of the ISO?
Ans: To promote the development of standardization and related activities in the world for easy international exchange of goods and services.

INTERNATIONAL ORGANIZATIONS AND HEADQUARTERS

International Monetary Fund (IMF): Washington DC (USA)
World Bank: Washington DC (USA)
International Bank for Reconstruction and Development (IBRD): Washington DC (USA)
General Agreement on Tariffs and Trade (GATT): Geneva (Switzerland)
World Trade organization (WTO): Geneva (Switzerland)
United Nations Conference on Trade and Development (UNCTAD): Geneva (Switzerland)
Asian Development Bank: Manila (Philippines)
South Asian Association for Regional Cooperation (SAARC): Kathmandu (Nepal)
Association of Southeast Asian Nations (ASEAN): Jakarta (Indonesia)
Organizations of the Petroleum Exporting Countries (OPEC): Vienna (Austria)
Food and Agriculture organization (FAO): Rome (Italy)
The United Nations Educational Scientific and Cultural organization (UNESCO): Paris (France)
International Labor Organization (ILO): Geneva (Switzerland)
Interpol: Lyons (France)
UNICEP: New York (USA)
United Nations Human Rights Commission (UNHRC): Geneva (Switzerland)

CODES IN BANKING INDUSTRY

IFSC (Indian Financial System Code): It is an alphanumeric code that uniquely identifies a bank-branch participating in the two main Electronic Funds Settlement Systems in India: The Real Time Gross Settlement (RTGS) and the National Electronic Funds Transfer (NEFT) Systems. It is an 11-character code assigned by Reserve Bank of India for the identification of the bank branches.

The components of IFS code are:
• The first four alphabetic characters representing the bank name,
• The fifth character is 0 (zero) and reserved for future use, and
• The last six characters (usually numeric but can be alphabetic) representing the branch.

Example: IFS Code of a branch of Punjab National Bank in Delhi is PUNB0614800.

MICR (Magnetic Ink Character Recognition)
A unique code used to identify the particular branch of a particular bank. It is used mainly by the banking industry to ease the processing and clearance of cheques and other documents. The technology allows MICR readers to scan and read the information directly into a data-collection device. Unlike barcodes and similar technologies, MICR characters can be read easily by humans. It is a 9-digit code.

The components of MICR code are:
• The first three digits represent the city code of the bank branch - generally the pin code initials,
• The next three digits represent the bank code, and
• The last three digits represent the bank branch.

Example: MICR-No of a branch of Punjab National Bank in Delhi is 110024490

BSR (Basic Statistical Returns)
• 7-digit code
• BSR code will be allotted to banks by Reserve Bank of India.Bank BSR code is not a branch code.BSR code will be assigned to each branch of a bank seperately to identify submission of returns to the RBI by Income Tax Department through online upload of challan details, named as OLTAS (Online Tax Accounting System).While filling TDS/TCS (tax deducted at source/ tax collected at source) returns, BSR code is used in details related to challan and deductee.

Example: BSR Code of a branch of Punjab National Bank in Delhi is 305066.

SWIFT (Society for Worldwide Interbank Financial Telecommunication)
8 to 11 Alphabetic code.
It is approved by the International Organization for Standardization (ISO). A SWIFT code is an internationally recognized bank code to identify the bank all over the world.
It is a Belgium based secure financial messaging service used by over 11,000 banking and securities organisations.
SWIFT Codes are used when transferring money between banks, particularly for international wire transfers, and also for the exchange of other messages between banks in a secure standardized and reliable environment.
SWIFT Code is required for overseas fund transfer for the particular bank.

Example: SWIFT Code of a branch of Punjab National Bank in Delhi is PUNBINBBDRG

*Note: Not all bank branches have individual SWIFT codes, so if it is not available for your branch, you can use the SWIFT code of a nearby branch of same bank. SWIFT code is also known as Bank Identifier Code (BIC).

SWIFT gpi:
The SWIFT Global Payment Initiative (gpi) is the latest initiative launched by SWIFT to improve customer banking experience in the world.

Permanent Account Number (PAN)
• 10-character alpha-numeric code
• It helps to identify the Indian nationals and regular Income Taxpayer under the Indian Income Tax Act, 1961.

• It is issued by the Indian Income Tax Department under the supervision of the Central Board for Direct Taxes (CBDT).
Income Tax PAN card will be issued under Section 139A of the Income Tax Act.

Tax Deduction and Collection Account Number (TAN)

10 Alpha Numeric code. It will be issued to persons who are requisite to deduct tax (TDS) or collect tax (TCS) on payments made by them under the Indian Income Tax Act, 1961.
• Without TAN number TDS/TCS returns will not be accepted.
• Challans for TDS/TCS payments will not be accepted by banks.
• iTAN is applied through "Form No. 49B" (prescribed under Indian Income Tax Law).

AADHAR

• 12-digit code
• An Aadhaar card is a 12-digit Unique Identification (UID) number. It is the biometric ID system.
• It is issued by the government of India to each citizen of the country.
• The Unique Identification Authority of India (UDAI under the Planning Commission of India, is responsible for managing Aadhaar numbers and Aadhaar identification cards.

Universal Account Number (UAN)

• 12-digit code
• A Universal Account Number (UAN) will be generated by Employees Provident Fund organization (EPFO) for each of the PF contributing members
• The number allows portability of PF accounts to claim or withdrawal of EPF balance. The UAN will act as an umbrella for the multiple Member Ids allotted to an individual by different establishments.

Permanent Retirement Account Number (PRAN)

• 12-digit code
• PRAN is a unique 12-digit number issued to the state and central employees to receive their pension throughout their life under the National Pension System (NPS) (This NPS scheme was launched in 2004). It is regulated by the Pension Fund Regulatory and Development Authority (PFRDA), created by an Act of the Parliament of India.
• The number remains active for the lifetime of a subscriber.

International Securities Identification Number (ISIN)

• 12 Alpha Numeric code.
• It is an international numbering system developed by the International Organization for Standardization (ISO) to number specific securities, such as stocks (equity and preference shares), bonds, options and futures and other settlements.
• First two digits - country code,
• Next nine digits - unique identification number for the security
• Last digit
- check digit
E.g- INA082B07072.

Legal Entity Identifier (LEI)

• 20-digit alpha numeric code
• The Legal Entity Identifier (LEl) is a 20-digit, alpha-numeric code developed by the International Organization for
Standardization (ISO). It is a key measure to improve the quality and accuracy of financial data systems for better risk management.

Mobile Money Identifier (MMID)

• 7-digit code
• It is issued by the bank to their Mobile Banking registered customers for availing IMPS service as a beneficiary. You will have different MMIDs for different accounts and all these could be linked to a single registered mobile number.
• First four digits - to identify the bank of the user
• Next three digits - to identify the account of the user.

CARD AND IDENTIFICATION NUMBER

Card security code: A card security code (CSC; also known as CVC, CVV, or several other names) is a series of numbers that, in addition to the bank card number, is printed (not embossed) on a credit or debit card. The CSC is used as a security feature for card not present transactions, where a personal identification number (PIN) cannot be manually entered by the cardholder (as they would during point-of-sale or card present transactions). It was instituted to reduce the incidence of credit card fraud.

The codes have different names and different countries and companies that uses.

"CSC" or "card security code": debit cards, American Express (three digits on back of card, also referred to as 3CSC)
"CVC" or "card validation code": Mastercard
"CVV" or "card verification value": Visa
"CAV" or "card authentication value": JCB
"CID": "card ID", "card identification number", or "card identification code": Discover, American Express
"CVD" or "card verification data": Discover
"CVE" or "Elo verification code": Elo in Brazil
"CVN" or "card validation number", also "card verification number": China UnionPay, Google Ads
"SPC" or "signature panel code"

History of cards

Credit cards were invented in 1946 CE by John Biggins.

In 1950, the Diners Club card became the first store card to gain widespread use after founder Frank McNamara was inspired by leaving his wallet at home while out dining. He and a partner, Ralph Schneider, launched the first Diners Club card, widely considered to be the birth of the modern charge card.

The concept of using a card for purchases was described in 1887 by Edward Bellamy in his utopian novel Looking Backward. Bellamy used the term credit card eleven times in this novel, although this referred to a card for spending a guaranteed minimum income, rather than borrowing, making it more similar to a debit card.

The Bank of Delaware in the US was the first to launch a pilot project involving Debit Cards in 1966. By the 1970s, many other banks started working on similar ideas. And by the 1980s-1990s, with the rising popularity of ATMs, Debit Card users grew exponentially.

Debit Cards is also known as Bank card or Check Card.

Visa Cards: Visa card is a payment network company that transfers the fund electronically all over the Globe.
It is the first multinational financial service provider company in California, the USA in 1958.
It also provides many financial services like a credit card, debit card and prepaid card to clients.

Master Cards: The master card company is located in New York, USA since 1966.
This company is earlier known as Interbank or Master charge.
It is a multinational payment technology network company that provides financial services to the customers.

BANKS BOARD BUREAU (BBB)

The Banks Board Bureau (BBB) is an autonomous body in India. It was established in 2016 by the Government of India. BBB's primary purpose is to improve the governance of public sector banks. It plays a crucial role in recommending appointments to top leadership positions in these banks. BBB aims to enhance the efficiency and performance of public sector banks. It recommends candidates for the positions of CEOs, executive directors, and non-executive chairpersons. The bureau also assesses the performance of bank executives and formulates strategies for their development. Overall, the Banks Board Bureau focuses on transforming the banking sector to meet contemporary challenges and improve its competitiveness.

History of Bank Board Bureau in India
1. The Bank Board Bureau was first recommended in May 2014 by the 'Committee to Review Governance of Boards of Banks in India' chaired by P.J. Nayak.

2. Based on the recommendations of the P.J. Nayak Committee, the Central Government in 2016, constituted the Bank Board Bureau as a part of the seven point 'Indradhanush Mission' to overhaul the functioning of the PSBs.

3. The first chairperson of the BBB which was constituted in February 2016 was the former Comptroller and Auditor General of India, Vinod Rai.

4. It is an autonomous recommendatory body and its headquarters are in Mumbai, Maharashtra.

5. The Bank Board Bureau functions as a replacement for the erstwhile Appointments Board of the Central Government.
It is a 'public authority' under the Right to Information Act, 2005.

PRIORITY SECTOR LENDING

Priority sector lending (PSL) is lending to those sectors of the economy which may not otherwise receive timely and adequate credit. This role is assigned by the RBI to the banks for providing a specified portion of the bank lending to a few specific sectors. This is essentially meant for an all-round development of the economy as opposed to focusing only on the financial sector.

History of PSL
The priority sector started gaining popularity in 1972, right after the National Credit Council's plea that commercial banks should give more emphasis to the priority sector.
Initially, in 1974, the commercial banks were given a target of 33.33% of their total credit should be driven towards the priority sector.
Following the recommendations of Dr K S Krishnaswamy Committee, this target was later revised to 40% of the total credit given by the banking institutions.

Categories of Priority Sectors

The Reserve Bank of India (RBI) has classified the following eight categories of priority sectors in India:
Agriculture
Micro, Small and Medium Enterprises (MSMEs)
Export Credit
Education
Housing
Social Infrastructure
Renewable Energy
Others

WHAT IS NON-PERFORMING ASSET (NPA) IN BANKING?

The NPA meaning in banking is any asset that fails to perform and cannot generate revenue for the bank. Loans are assets for banks as the interest that the borrower pays to the bank is their source of income. Any consumer who fails to pay the interest is categorized as "non-performing" by the bank as they fail to meet their obligations.

How does Non-Performing Assets (NPA) Work?
When a non-payment of interest arises, the borrower is forced to liquidate any assets pledged as a part of the debt agreement.

For example, assume a company borrows a loan of Rs 2,00,000 and makes a monthly payment of Rs 2,000. But due to some operational failure, the company cannot process payments, which have been due for the past 3 months. The bank will then classify this loan as a non-performing asset. Such non-payment of the loan causes a significant burden to the lenders.

The non-performing assets reduce the income for the banks or financial institutions and cause the decreases in earnings to be disrupted. They negatively impact the balance sheet.

Categories of non-performing assets
Depending on the duration of the assets that have remained static or have not performed for more than 90 days, they are classified into various categories.

1. Sub-standard asset: A non-performing asset that is overdue for less than or equal to 12 months is a Sub-standard asset.

2. Doubtful assets: It is an asset that has remained NPA for more than 12 months.

3. Loss Asset: An asset that remains a non-performing asset for more than 3 years is a loss asset. This occurs when a bank faces total loss as it cannot recover the asset.

Asset Reconstruction Company: A specialized financial institution that buys the NPAs or Bad Loans from banks so that the latter can clean up their balance sheet. ARCs are the business of buying bad loans from Banks. Banks rather than going after their defaulters by wasting time and efforts can sell the bad assets to ARCs at a mutually agreed price.

SARFAESI ACT, 2002

SARFAESI Act stands for the Securitization and Reconstruction of Financial Assets and Enforcement of Security Interest Act of 2002. It is a legislative act passed by the parliament of India in the year 2002. It empowers lenders, which include banks and other financial institutions, to recover bad loans efficiently.

History of SARFAESI Act, 2002

In 1991, Narasimham Committee – I (Committee on the Financial System) observed that borrowers obtain stay orders from ordinary courts, so banks and financial institutions face difficulty while recovering Non-Performing Assets(NPAs). Hence, to strengthen this process, Debt Recovery Tribunals were set up in 1993, and the loan recovery process was made beyond the jurisdiction of ordinary courts.

In 1998, Narasimham Committee – II (Committee on Banking Sector Reforms) observed that Debt Recovery Tribunals (DRTs) need to be strengthened with a law, So, Securitization and Reconstruction of Financial Assets and Enforcement of Security Interest (SARFAESI) Act enacted in the 2002.

What is the SARFAESI Act, 2002?
Ans: The SARFAESI Act, 2002 stands for the Securitization and Reconstruction of Financial Assets and Enforcement of Security Interest Act, 2002, It is a law that authorises banks and financial institutions to enforce security interests and recover non-performing assets without approaching civil courts.

a. If a borrower defaults on a secured loan, the lender can seize and auction residential or commercial properties pledged as security, except agricultural land, which is exempt.
b. The Act applies only to secured loans backed by assets such as mortgages, pledges, or hypothecation.
c. For unsecured loans, banks must approach the civil courts to initiate recovery.

By streamlining the asset recovery process, SARFAESI helps reduce delays in handling defaults and improves overall credit discipline in the financial system.

Why was the SARFAESI Act Introduced?
Ans: The SARFAESI Act, 2002 was introduced to provide a legal framework for the securitization and reconstruction of financial assets, and for the enforcement of security interests by banks and financial institutions.

It was designed to facilitate faster recovery of loans and reduce the burden of non-performing assets (NPAs). The Act extends to the entire country and covers all matters related to or incidental to its main objectives.

Amendment:
In 2016, the SARFAESI Act was amended through the Enforcement of Security Interest and Recovery of Debts Laws and Miscellaneous Provisions (Amendment) Act, 2016. This amendment aimed to strengthen the recovery process and improve the legal framework for debt resolution. The 2016 amendment impacted four key legislations:
The SARFAESI Act, 2002
The Recovery of Debts Due to Banks and Financial Institutions Act, 1993 (RDDBFI)
The Indian Stamp Act, 1899
The Depositories Act, 1996
These amendments were made to streamline asset recovery procedures and enhance the effectiveness of secured lending in India.

Objectives of SARFAESI Act, 2002
The key objectives of the SARFAESI Act include the following:
a. Efficient or rapid recovery of non-performing assets (NPAs) of the banks and FIs.
b. Allows banks and financial institutions to auction properties (say, commercial/residential) when the borrower fails to repay their loans.

Who does the SARFAESI Act Apply to?
The SARFAESI Act, 2002 applies primarily to banks, financial institutions, and Asset Reconstruction Companies (ARCs). Below is a simplified overview of its scope:

I. Banks and Financial Institutions
a. Can enforce secured loans without court intervention.
b. Must classify borrower accounts as Non-Performing Assets (NPAs) as per RBI guidelines.
c. Can appeal to the Debts Recovery Tribunal (DRT) and Appellate Tribunal if challenged.

II. Asset Reconstruction Companies (ARCs)
a. Must be registered with the Reserve Bank of India (RBI).
b. Can acquire financial assets from banks and issue security receipts to qualified buyers.
c. Allowed to restructure assets, change management, or enforce security interests.
d. Recognized as Public Financial Institutions under this Act.

III. Central Government Powers
a. Can set up a Central Registry for transactions involving securitization or asset reconstruction.
b. May extend the Act's provisions to Non-Banking Financial Companies (NBFCs) and other entities.

IV. Scope Limitations
The Act does not apply to:
a. Agricultural land
b. Loans under ₹1 lakh
c. Cases where 80% of the loan has already been repaid

Role of SARFAESI Act, 2002
The SARFAESI Act, 2002 plays a critical role in strengthening India's banking and financial system. Its key roles are outlined below.

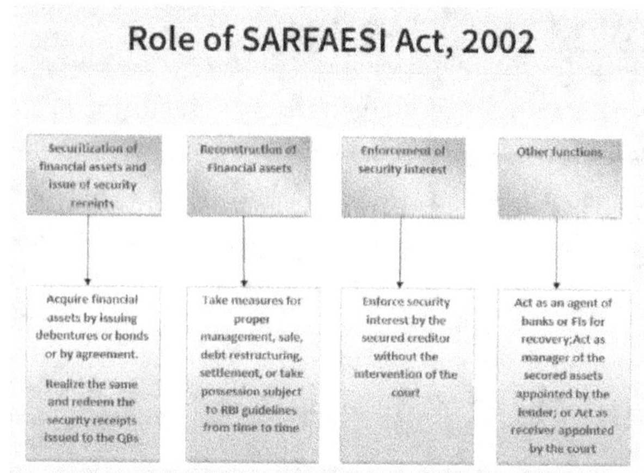

How does the SARFAESI Act, 2002 Work?
SARFAESI Act, 2002 provides power to a bank or financial institution to seize the property of a defaulting borrower. If the loan borrowers make any default in repayment of a loan or a loan installment, the financial institution can classify the account as Non-Performing Asset (NPA).
The banks or financial institutions can issue notices to the defaulting borrowers to discharge their liabilities within 60 days period. When the defaulting borrower fails to comply with the bank or financial institution notice, then the SARFAESI Act gives the following recourse to a bank:
a. Take possession of the loan security
b. Lease, sell or assign the right to security.
c. Manage the same or appoint any person to manage the same.
The Act also provides for the establishment of ARCs, regulated by the RBI, to acquire assets from banks and other financial institutions.

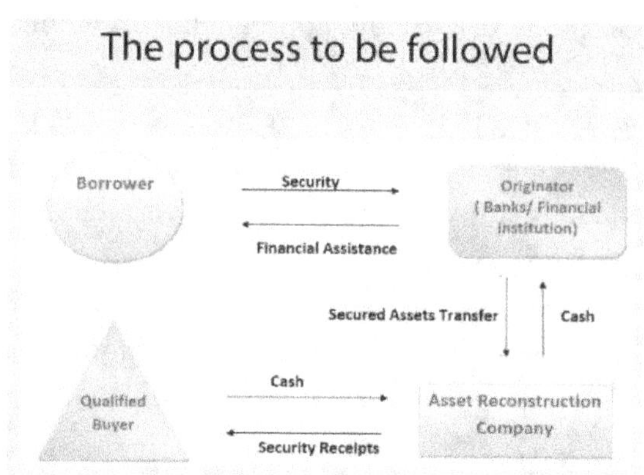

Methods of Recovery Under SARFAESI Act, 2002. The SARFAESI Act provides the following three methods of recovery of the Non-Performing Assets (NPAs):

I. Securitisation

a. Securitisation is the process of issuing marketable securities backed by a pool of existing assets such as home or auto loans. An asset can be sold after it is converted into marketable security.

b. A securitisation or asset reconstruction company can raise funds from only the Qualified Institutional Buyers (QIBs) by forming schemes for acquiring financial assets.

II. Asset Reconstruction

a. Asset reconstruction empowers asset reconstruction companies.

b. It can be done by managing the borrower's business by selling or acquiring it or by rescheduling payments of debt payable by the borrower as per the provisions of the Act.

III. Enforcement of security without the interruption of the court

a. The Act empowers banks and financial institutions to issue notices to individuals who have obtained a secured asset from the borrower for paying the due amount and claim to a borrower's debtor to pay the sum due to the borrower.

Assets Not Covered Under SARFAESI Act, 2002. The SARFAESI Act does not cover the following assets:

a. Money or security issued under the Sale of Goods Act, 1930 or Indian Contract Act, 1872.

b. Any lease, hire-purchase, conditional sale, or any other contract where no security interest has been created.

c. Any rights of the unpaid seller under Section 47 of the Sale of Goods Act, 1930.

d. Any properties which are not liable for sale or attachment under Section 60 of the Code of Civil Procedure, 1908.

The SARFAESI Act, 2002 provides banks with a powerful legal mechanism to recover secured loan dues efficiently while balancing borrower rights. Understanding the SARFAESI Act, its applicability, recovery process, and safeguards helps borrowers and lenders navigate loan defaults and enforcement actions with greater clarity.

Section 29 of the SARFAESI Act, 2002, outlines penalties for offenses, stating that any person who contravenes attempts to contravene, or abets the contravention of the Act or its rules can be punished with imprisonment for up to one year, a fine, or both. This section ensures compliance with the act's provisions regarding NPA recovery.

Key Aspects of Section 29 (Offences & Penalties):

Scope: Applies to any person contravening the provisions of the SARFAESI Act, 2002, or any rules made under it.

Punishment: The offense is punishable by imprisonment for a term extending to one year, a fine, or both.

Context: This section acts as a deterrent against obstructing or violating the legal process allowed to bank for taking possession of secured assets.

Section 32 of the SARFAESI Act, 2002, provides statutory protection (protection of action taken in good faith) to the Reserve Bank of India (RBI), the Central Registry, secured creditors (banks/FIs), and their officers. It bars legal proceedings, suits, or prosecutions against them for actions done in good faith under the Act.

Key Aspects of Section 32:

Protection Scope: It ensures that officials are not personally liable for actions, such as seizing or selling assets taken in accordance with the Act.

"Good Faith" Constraint: The protection is not absolute; it only applies to actions done honestly and with due care. It does not protect against malicious actions or harassment.

Legal Standing: It serves as a defense in court but generally cannot be used to prevent an investigation at the preliminary stage.

Part of Chapter VI: It falls under the "Miscellaneous" chapter of the Act.

PROMPT CORRECTIVE ACTION (PCA)

Prompt Corrective Action (PCA) is a framework under which banks with weak financial metrics are put under watch by the Reserve Bank of India (RBI).

The RBI introduced the PCA framework in 2002 as a structured early-intervention mechanism for banks that become undercapitalized due to poor asset quality, or vulnerable due to loss of profitability.

It aims to check the problem of Non-Performing Assets (NPAs) in the Indian banking sector.

Monitored Areas:
Capital, Asset Quality and Capital-To-Risk Weighted Assets Ratio (CRAR), NPA ratio, Tier I Leverage Ratio, will be the key areas for monitoring in the revised framework.

Note: The Capital Adequacy Ratio, also known as capital-to-risk weighted assets ratio (CRAR), is used to protect depositors and promote the stability and efficiency of financial systems around the world.

WHAT ARE BASEL NORMS?

Basel norms or Basel accords are the international banking regulations issued by the Basel Committee on Banking Supervision.

The Basel norms is an effort to coordinate banking regulations across the globe, with the goal of strengthening the international banking system.

It is the set of the agreement by the Basel committee of Banking Supervision which focuses on the risks to banks and the financial system.

What is the Basel committee on Banking Supervision?
The Basel Committee on Banking Supervision (BCBS) is the primary global standard setter for the prudential regulation of banks and provides a forum for regular cooperation on banking supervisory matters for the central banks of different countries. It was established by the Central Bank governors of the Group of Ten countries in 1974.

The committee expanded its membership in 2009 and then again in 2014. The BCBS now has 45 members from 28 Jurisdictions, consisting of Central Banks and authorities with responsibility of banking regulation. It provides a forum for regular cooperation on banking supervisory matters. Its objective is to enhance understanding of key supervisory issues and improve the quality of banking supervision worldwide.

Why these norms?
a. Banks lend to different types of borrowers, and each carries its own risk.
b. They lend the deposits of the public as well as money raised from the market, i.e, equity and debt.
c. This exposes the bank to a variety of risks of default and as a result they fall at times.
Therefore, Banks have to keep aside a certain percentage of capital as security against the risk of non – recovery. The Basel committee has produced norms called Basel Norms for Banking to tackle this risk.

Why the name Basel?
Basel is a city in Switzerland.
It is the headquarters of the Bureau of International Settlement (BIS), which fosters cooperation among central banks with a common goal of financial stability and common standards of banking regulations.
It was founded in 1930.
The Basel Committee on Banking Supervision is housed in the BIS offices in Basel, Switzerland.

What are these norms?
The Basel Committee has issued three sets of regulations which are known as Basel-I, II, and III.

India adopted Basel-I guidelines in 1999.

Note: Bank run: It occurs when a large number of customers of a bank or other financial institution withdraw their deposits simultaneously over concerns of the bank's solvency. As more people withdraw their funds, the probability of default increases, prompting more people to withdraw their deposits.

DISINVESTMENT

Disinvestment refers to an act of an organisation or the government of a state to raise funds by selling ownership stake. The sale can also be a liquidation of asset or stake in a subsidiary of an organisation or government undertaking.

In many instances, disinvestment occurs as a policy decision of the government when a state government decides to transfer the ownership and management of undertakings to private hands.

The aim of disinvestment is to facilitate re-allocation of funds or resources to better use or monetise assets. Disinvestment also helps in lowering debt and restructuring of business. The process helps in increasing the return on investment.

Eg: As per Money control news (02 Feb 2024), Currently the government holds a controlling 57.49 percent stake in SBI and 58.89 percent stake in ONGC. Means the government has the majority shares or ownership ie, more than 50%. But the government is open to the idea of disinvestment of equity stake in blue-chip PSUs including State Bank of India (SBI) and Oil and Natural Gas Corp (ONGC). The government is not against the idea of holding a minority stake (less than 50 percent) in key strategic public sector companies. Like the government has sold the controlling stake in Air India which was acquired by Tata Group.

The government does all the disinvestment through the department called Department of Investment and Public Asset Management (DIPAM). It deals with all matters relating to management of Central Government investments in equity including disinvestment of equity in Central Public Sector Undertakings. The three major areas of its work relate to Strategic Disinvestment and Privatization, Minority Stake Sales and Capital Restructuring. All matters relating to sale of Central Government equity through offer for sale or private placement or any other mode in the Central Public Sector Undertakings as well as strategic disinvestment of CPSEs is dealt with in DIPAM. DIPAM is a Department under the Ministry of Finance.

The Department of Disinvestment was set up as a separate Department on 10th December 1999 and was later renamed as Ministry of Disinvestment form 6th September 2001. From 27th May 2004, the Department of Disinvestment is one of the Departments under the Ministry of Finance. The Department of Disinvestment has been renamed as Department of Investment and Public Asset Management (DIPAM) from 14th April 2016.

FINANCIAL TERMS

1. DEAF: Depositor Education Awareness Fund maintained by RBI

2. ASBA: Application Supported by Blocked Amount; this is a procedure used by online portfolio companies like zerodha, grow etc for selling of shares to the individuals. And the facility is provided by the banks to investors in Initial Public Offering (IPO), Follow on Public offers (FPO) in share market and New Fund offers (NFO) in mutual funds.

3. Currency Chest: It is operated by RBI to provide good quality currency notes to the customers. RBI appoints commercial banks to open and monitor currency chest on behalf of RBI where there is no regional branch of RBI or where the commercial bank is huge.

4. CIBIL: Credit Information Bureau of India Ltd maintains the borrower history. Whenever a person applies for loans or credit cards the person's credit worthiness is checked through CIBIL score.

5. Cheque Truncation System (CTS): It is a cheque clearing system undertaken by RBI for faster clearance. With this the physical flow of cheque stopped and send electronically.

6. Lead Bank Scheme: under this scheme all the nationalised banks and some private sector banks are given lead role in a particular area for the economic development of the area.

7. UPI was launched in April 2016. UPI needs Virtual Payment Address (VPA) to transfer money.

8. JAM Trinity: Jan Dhan Account, Aadhar Card and Mobile

9. Block Chain Banking: It is used behind cryptocurrency.

10. Automated Clearing House (ACH): An Automated Clearing House (ACH) is an electronic network that manages electronic banking transactions. Any entity (business, government organization, or individual) can use the ACH network to send or receive funds. Employers typically use ACH to pay their employees through direct deposits. The ACH network is regulated by the federal government and managed by the National Automated Clearing House Association (NACHA).

11. M-Cap: Market Capitalisation which is Number of shares in market * Price of shares at the end of the day.

12. Prime Customers: Customer beneficial to bank.

13. Base Rate: Interest rate, the minimum, not to go below that rate.

14. BASE / BASIC salary: Minimum Salary, atleast that is base.

15. Surcharge: Additional tax taken on a tax already paid.

16. Cess: Tax on Tax

17. First payment bank of India: Airtel Payment Bank (Rajasthan 2016)

18. Second payment bank of India: India Post Payment Bank (Ranchi)

19. Third payment bank of India: Paytm Payment Bank

20. CASA: Current Account and Savings Account

21. RAFA: Recurring Deposit A/c & Fixed Deposit A/c

22. ICMIS: Integrated Cooperative Management Information System.

23. RDA: Recommended Dearness Allowance

24. UDAN: Ude Desh Ka Aam Nagrik

25. DBT: Direct Benefit Transfer

26. ZUUL: API Gateway

27. SEZ: Special Economic Zone formed under SEZ Act 2005. First Export Promotion Zone (EPZ) is Kandla.

28. Teaser rates: Banks offer teaser rates for home loans. Which is the trailer of the main loan.

29. Hot Money: It is a currency that moves regularly and quickly between financial markets. So, investors ensure they are getting the highest short-term interest rates available.

30. CAR: Capital Adequacy Ratio; given by committee named Basel Committee on Banking Supervision (BCBS). It means banks capital and risk attached to bank capital.

31. CRAR: Capital to Risk Weighted Asset Ratio

32. FCCB: Foreign Currency Convertible Bond

33. Brokers & Jobbers in share market: Jobber may be an Individual or organization that provides job. Jobber provides shares for sell or buy to the brokers. And Brokers provides buy or sell shares to the customers.

34. Merger: Two companies form one. Name of two companies will be there. Eg, Vodafone + Idea= Vodafone Idea

35. Acquisition: when a company takes control of the other company. Big companies acquire smaller companies. Eg: Microsoft acquire LinkedIn.

36. Amalgamation: when two or more companies merge. Combining in wider sense. Name of one company survives.
Eg: SBI And SBI Associates

37. Bad Loans / PARA: Public Asset Rehabilitation Agency. A bad bank separates good and bad assets of a bank. It means separates Performing asset and Non-Performing Asset.

38. D stands for DNS for NEFT and DNS means Deferred Net Settlement means no Real time payment that no immediate payment.

39. NACH: National Automated Clearing House. This application provides platform for regular and bulk payments.
Eg, A company gives salary on the same day to all the employees using NACH that deducts salary automatically from the company's account. Also used for EMI payments. Also called Auto Debit or Auto Pay. Earlier called Electronic Clearing Service. Regulated by NPCI.

40. Cryptocurrency: Centralized Digital Currency.

41. CERT: Computer Emergency Response Team

42. NFS: National Financial Switch is the largest interconnected network of ATMs.

43. _____ charge or fee is imposed on merchants by bank for accepting payment from their customers in Cr and Dr cards every timecard is used for payment.
Ans: MDR (Merchant Discount Rate)

44. D-SIB: Domestic Systematically Important Banks. Banks which are too big to fail.

45. National Rural Health Mission: 2005

46. Midday Meal Scheme: 1995

47. Prime Minister Employment Generation Programme (PMEGP): 2008

48. Mahatma Gandhi National Rural Employment Gurantee Act (MGNREGA): 2005

49. NREGA: 2006

50. Acquihiring: A buys stake in B that is acquisition. A takes main employees from B is acquihiring.

51. Currency Swap: Agreement between two countries in terms of exchange of currencies. Eg: If India needs US Dollars, USA will provide to India at some %. If USA needs Rupee, India will provide.

52. Helicopter Money: During the Europe and Japan recession the term was coined in Europe. Government will give money to people to spend. Government sells securities to the RBI and gets money further spread those money to people for spending.

53. Intellectual Property:
Patents: The Government gives right to the owner to exclude others from using, producing, selling the product.

Trademark: A sign design which makes it easier to differentiate from other products.

Copyright: The Government created right for a limited period of time.

54. Gyan Sangam: It is known as merger of banks.

55. De dollarization: Less usage of dollars by any country. If RBI increases Gold Reserves and decreases reserves of dollars.

56. NBFC: Non-Banking Finance Company

57. Gold Schemes:
Gold Sovereign Bond: Issued by RBI on behalf of the Government. Minimum charges. Better Liquidity.

Gold Monetization scheme: It is a deposit scheme by banks where you will be paid interest on the gold you give. Minimum deposit of gold is 30 gms. Income tax free.

58. Protectionism: Also called Anti Dumping Duty. A policy by the Indian Government to safeguard the Indian manufacturers from foreign cheap goods.

Indian manufacturers: Goods: Rs 50
China manufacturers: Goods: Rs 20
Now Indian government will add anti dumping duty / tax of Rs 30 in India on the Chinese goods to make it equal. So that Indian manufacturers donot suffer.

59. Sec 22 of Banking Regulations Act 1949: Licensing of Banks.

60. Financial and Share Market

(a) Escrow Account: Temporary pass through an Account by 3rd parties during transaction between two parties.

A. (Shareholder) ————————————> Company
               Buys a share

Till the time A doesn't gets the share the amount is with the third party. As soon as A gets the share, company receives the payment.

(b) Gilt Edged Securities: High Secured Government securities.

(c) Stock (paper): A security representating the ownership of a company.

A Company: 5 Shares of Rs 100 to Mr Binod. Here each unit is called Share.

(d) Share: Each unit of stock is called Share. Eg: Ramesh holds 80,000 shares of stock in a company.

(e) Stake: Ramesh owns 80,000 shares which is 8% of the total stock of the 100,000 shares. That means Ramesh holds 80% stake in the company.

(f) Bond: Bond has fixed interest and fixed time period and is issued for taking loans.
Government issues Bond while other high rated companies issues Debentures. Both are same but Government issues are called BOND while Companies issues are called DEBENTURES.

(g) Bull Market: Financial market in which share prices are rising or expected to rise.

(h) Bearish Market: Financial market in which share prices are expected to fall.

(I) Commodity money: Whose value comes from currency of which it is made. (Having Intrinsic Value). Eg Gold, Silver, Coffee, Whear, Rice.

(j) Fiat Money: Doesn't have intrinsic value. Value decided by the government. Eg: on 8 Nov 2016, Old Rs 500 note have value of Rs 500. But on 9 Nov 2016 Old Rs 500 note has zero value.

(k) Representative Money: Gold, Silver, Tobacco

(l) Purchasing power parity (ppp):

Purchasing Power Parity (PPP)
(Shows cost of living)

Which Salary is better?

USA: Rs 1cr (approx 125000$)   INDIA: Rs 30 Lakhs

Burger Cost:

USA: 4 $ that means it should cost in India Rs 320. (1$ = Rs 80, 4$×80) (considering no labour and transportation cost)
But the Actual rate in India is Rs 60/-

Economy is related to Cost of Living Index.

In USA its 4$, In India its Rs 60, if we compare the price the rate comes out and that rate is called Purchasing Power Parity.

PPP Rate= Price 1/ Price 2 = 60/4 = 15/4 = 1$ is equal to Rs 15

1$ = Rs 80 is the market trade / trading rate / exchange rate. But the actual rate of real prices is called PPP.

Like as per PPP 1$ = Rs 15/-

NATIONAL ORGANISATION

Reserve Bank of India (RBI): It is India's central bank and regulatory body under the jurisdiction of Ministry of Finance, Government of India. It commenced its operations on 1 April 1935 in accordance with the Reserve Bank of India Act, 1934. It is Headquartered in Mumbai. Following India's independence on 15 August 1947, the RBI was nationalized on 1 January 1949. Sir Osborne Smith was the first Governor of the Reserve Bank

Issue of Currency: For the printing of notes, RBI uses four facilities.

The Security Printing and Minting Corporation of India Limited (SPMCIL), a wholly owned company of the Government of India, has printing presses at Nashik, Maharashtra and Dewas, Madhya Pradesh.

The Bharatiya Reserve Bank Note Mudran Private Limited (BRBNMPL), owned by the RBI, has printing facilities in Mysore, Karnataka and Salboni, West Bengal.

For the minting of coins, SPMCIL has four mints at Mumbai, Noida, Kolkata and Hyderabad for coin production.

Securities and Exchange Board of India (SEBI): It is the regulatory body for securities and commodity market in India under the jurisdiction of Ministry of Finance, Government of India. It was established on 12 April 1988 and given Statutory Powers on 30 January 1992 through the SEBI Act, 1992. It is headquartered in Mumbai. The SEBI is managed by a total of 9 members, which consists of the following: First, the chairman is nominated by the Union Government of India. Two members, ie., Officers from the Union Finance Ministry.
One member from the Reserve Bank of India.
The remaining five members are nominated by the Union Government of India, out of them at least three shall be whole-time members.

Pension Fund Regulatory and Development Authority: It is the regulatory body under the jurisdiction of Ministry of Finance, Government of India for overall supervision and regulation of pension in India. On 23 August 2003, Interim Pension Fund Regulatory & Development Authority (PFRDA) was established through a resolution by the Government of India to promote, develop and regulate the pension sector in India.

On 19 September 2013, the President, Pranab Mukherjee, gave his assent to the Pension Fund Regulatory and Development Authority Bill of 2013.

This improved, foolproof and re-approved Bill, with the acceptance of all political parties in India, has replaced the old and imperfect IPRDA Bill of 2003. Headquarters - New Delhi

The Authority consists of a Chairperson and not more than six members, of whom at least three shall be whole-time members, to be appointed by the Central Government.

National Bank for Agriculture and Rural Development (NABARD): It is an apex regulatory body for overall regulation and licensing of regional rural banks and apex cooperative banks in India.

NABARD was established on the recommendations of B. Sivaramman Committee on 12 July 1982 to implement the National Bank for Agriculture and Rural Development Act 1981. It replaced the Agricultural Credit Department (ACD) and Rural Planning and Credit Cell (RPCC) of Reserve Bank of India, and Agricultural Refinance and Development Corporation (ARDC). NABARD has its head office in Mumbai

Small Industries Development Bank of India: It is the apex regulatory body in India for overall regulation and licensing of microfinance institutions in India. It is under the jurisdiction of Ministry of

Finance. It was established on 2 April 1990, through an Act of Parliament. It is headquartered in Lucknow. Its purpose is to provide refinance facilities and short-term lending to industries, and serves as the principal financial institution in the Micro, Small and Medium Enterprises (MSME) sector.

National Housing Bank: It is the apex regulatory body for overall regulation and licensing of housing finance companies in India. It is under the jurisdiction of Ministry of Finance. It was set up on 9 July 1988 under the National Housing Bank Act, 1987.

NHB is wholly owned by Govt. of India as after 24 April 2019 notification of RBI, which contributed the entire paid-up capital. The Head office of NHB is at New Delhi.

Telecom Regulatory Authority of India: It is a statutory body set up by the Government of India. It was established on 20 February 1997 by an Act of Parliament to regulate telecom services and tariffs in India. It is headquartered in New Delhi

Food Safety and Standards Authority of India (FSSAI): It is a statutory body established under the Ministry of Health & Family Welfare. FSSAI was established on 5 August 2011 under Food
Safety and Standards Act, 2006. FSSAI is responsible for protecting and promoting public health through the regulation and supervision of food safety. The FSSAI has its headquarters at New Delhi.

National Association of Software and Service Companies (NASSCOM): It is an Indian non-governmental trade association and advocacy group focused mainly on Information Technology (IT) and Business Process Outsourcing (BPO) industry. Established on 1 March 1988, NASSCOM is a non-profit organisation. NASSCOM organizes the Indian Leadership Forum. It is headquartered in New Delhi

Associated Chambers of Commerce and Industry of India: It is a non-governmental trade association and advocacy group based in New Delhi, India ASSOCHAM was established in 1920 by promoter chambers, representing all regions of India.
The Association's head office is located in New Delhi ASSOCHAM members represent the following sectors:
A. Trade (national and international)
B. Industry (domestic and international)
C. Professionals (e.g. CAs, CMAs, lawyers, consultants)

Competition Commission of India: It is the competition regulator in India. It is a statutory body of the Government of India responsible for enforcing The Competition Act, 2002. It was established on 14 October 2003. It became fully functional in May 2009 with Dhanendra Kumar as its first Chairman.

It is the duty of the Commission to eliminate practices having adverse effect on competition, promote and sustain competition, protect the interests of consumers and ensure freedom of trade in the markets of India. HQ - New Delhi

Council of Scientific and Industrial Research (CSIR): The Council of Scientific and Industrial Research abbreviated as SIR was established by the Government of India on 26 September 1942.

Although it is mainly funded by the Ministry of Science and Technology, it operates as an autonomous body through the Societies Registration Act, 1860. It is headquartered in New Delhi. The research and development activities of SIR include aerospace engineering, structural engineering, ocean sciences, life sciences, metallurgy, chemicals, mining, food, petroleum, leather, and environmental science.
Organization Structure
• President: Prime Minister (Ex-Officio)
• Vice President: Minister of Science & Technology, India (Ex-Officio)

• Governing Body: The Director General is the head of the governing body.

The Shanti Swarup Bhatnagar Prize was established by CSIR in 1958. The prize is named after the Founder Director Shanti Swarup Bhatnagar.

Central Statistics Office: It is a governmental agency in India under the Ministry of Statistics and Programme Implementation. The CSO is located in Delhi. It is responsible for coordination of statistical activities in India and evolving and maintaining statistical standards.

The CSO was set up in the cabinet secretariat on 2 May 1951 as a part of the cabinet Secretariat and having coordinating and advisory functions.

At that time the name of CSO was Central Statistical Institute. In 1954 the CSI merged with CSO, and the new name was Central Statistical Organization. Recently, for a third time its name changed and now it called as Central Statistics Office.

Central Pollution Control Board: It is a statutory organization under the Ministry of Environment, Forest and Climate Change (Mo.E.F.C.C.). It was established on 22 September 1974 under the Water (Prevention and Control of Pollution) Act, 1974. The CPCB is also entrusted with the powers and functions under the Air (Prevention and Control of Pollution) Act, 1981. CPCB has its head office in New Delhi, with seven zonal offices and 5 laboratories.

Central Board of Film Certification: It is a statutory film-certification body in the Ministry of Information and Broadcasting of the Government of India.
Formation - 15 January 1951
Headquarters - Mumbai, Maharashtra
It is tasked with "regulating the public exhibition of films under the provisions of the Cinematograph Act 1952.

Geological Survey of India: It was founded in 1851, is a Government of India Ministry of Mines organization. GSI, headquartered at Kolkata. It was formed by East India Company in 1951. It is the second oldest survey in India after Survey of India (founded in 1767), for conducting geological surveys and studies of India,

Survey of India: The Survey of India is India's central engineering agency in charge of mapping and surveying. Set up in 1767 to help consolidate the territories of the British East India Company. The Survey of India, headquartered at Dehradun

Indian Council of Medical Research (ICMR): It is the apex body in India for the formulation, coordination and promotion of biomedical research. The ICMR is funded by the Government of India through the Department of Health Research, Ministry of Health and Family Welfare.
HQs - New Delhi
In 1911, the Government of India set up the Indian Research Fund Association (IRFA). After independence, several important changes were made in the organisation and the activities of the IRFA. It was redesignated the Indian Council of Medical Research (ICMR) in 1949, considerably expanded scope of functions

Insurance Regulatory Development Authority of India (IRDAI): It is a regulatory body under the jurisdiction of the Ministry of Finance. The agency's headquarters are in Hyderabad, Telangana, where it moved from Delhi in 2001. It was constituted by the Insurance Regulatory and Development Authority Act, 1999, an Act of Parliament passed by the Government of India. Following the recommendations of the Malhotra Committee, in 1999 the Insurance Regulatory and Development Authority (IRDA) was constituted to regulate and develop the insurance industry and was incorporated in April 2000.

Indian Council of Agricultural Research (ICAR): It is an autonomous body responsible for coordinating agricultural education and research in India. It reports to the Department of Agricultural Research and Education, Ministry of Agriculture. Formerly known as Imperial Council of Agricultural Research, it was established on 16 July 1929 as a registered society under the Societies Registration Act, 1860. The ICAR has its headquarters at New Delhi. With 101 ICAR institutes and 71 agricultural universities spread across the country, this is one of the largest national agricultural systems in the world.

Inland Waterways Authority of India (IWAI): It is the statutory authority in charge of the waterways in India. It was constituted under IWAI Act-1985 by parliament of India. It was was created by Government of India on 27 October 1986 for development and regulation of Inland waterways for shipping and navigation. Its headquarters is located in Noida, UP

Life Insurance Corporation: It is an Indian government owned insurance and investment corporation. It is under the ownership of Ministry of Finance. It was was established on September 1, 1956, when the Parliament of India passed the Life Insurance of India Act 1956 that nationalized the insurance industry in India. Over 245 insurance companies and provident societies were merged to create the state-owned Life Insurance Corporation of India
HOs - Mumbai

General Insurance Corporation of India: It is abbreviated as GIC Re and is a reinsurance company. It is under the ownership of Ministry of Finance, Government of India. It was incorporated on 22 November 1972 under Companies Act, 1956. HQ - Mumbai

National Medical Commission: It is an Indian regulatory body of 33 members which regulates medical education and medical professionals. It replaced the Medical Council of India on 25 September 2020. It was earlier established for 6 months by an ordinance in January 2019 and later became a permanent law passed by Parliament of India and later approved by President of India on 8 August 2019. The NITI Aayog had recommended the replacement of Medical Council of India (MCI) with National Medical Commission (NMC). Headquarters - New Delhi

National Safety Council (India): It is a premier, non-profit, self-financing and tripartite apex body at the national level in India. It is an autonomous body, which was set up by the Government of India, Ministry of Labour and Employment on 4 March 1966. The Set up to generate, develop and sustain a voluntary movement on Safety, Health and Environment (SHE) at the national level. It was registered as a Society under the Societies Registration Act, 1860 and subsequently, as a Public Trust under the Bombay Public Trust Act, 1950.

National Council of Educational Research and Training (NCERT): The Government of India's Ministry of Education resolved on 27 July 1961 to establish the National Council of Educational Research and Training, which formally began operation on 1 September 1961. It is established under the Societies' Registration Act. Its headquarters are located at Sri Aurobindo Marg in New Delhi.

It was established with the agenda to design and support a common system of education which is national in character and also enables and encourages the diverse culture across the country.

All India Council for Technical Education (AICTE): AICTE is a statutory body, and a national-level council for technical education, under the Department of Higher Education. Established in November 1945 first as an advisory body and later on in 1987 given statutory status by an Act of Parliament. AICTE is responsible for proper planning and coordinated development of the technical education and management education system in India. The AICTE has its new headquarters building in Delhi

Union Public Service Commission (UPSC): It is India's premier central recruiting agency for central government public servants.

Established on 1 October 1926 as Public Service Commission, it was later reconstituted as Federal Public Service Commission by the Government of India Act 1935; only to be renamed as today's Union Public Service Commission after the independence. The commission is headquartered in New Delhi and functions through its own secretariat. The agency's charter is granted by Part XIV of the Constitution of India, titled as Services Under the Union and the States. It is responsible for appointments to and examinations for Group A & Group B posts under civil services cadre and defence services cadre of central government.

National Research Development Corporation (NRDC): It was established in 1953 by the Government of India. Hq: New Delhi. It is presently working under the administrative control of the Dept. of Scientific & Industrial Research, Ministry of Science & Technology.

It was established with the primary objective to promote, develop and commercialize the technologies / know-how / inventions / patents / processes emanating from various national R&D institutions / Universities

Press Council of India: It is a statutory, adjudicating organization in India formed in 1966 by its parliament. Headquarters: New Delhi

Sports Authority of India (SAI): It is an apex national sports body of India for the development of sport in India. The Sports Authority of India originated with the committee formed to host the 1982 Asian Games in New Delhi.
On 25 January 1984, "Sports Authority of India" was established as a registered society by the "Department of Sports'" of Government of India's Ministry of Youth Affairs and Sports. Headquarters: SAI (Head office), Jawaharlal Nehru Stadium (Delhi),

SAI runs following two academic institutes that run graduate and post-graduate courses in sports medicine, sports and physical education.
Netaji Subhas National Institute of Sports (NSNIS) at Patiala
Lakshmibai National College of Physical Education (LNCPE) at Thiruvananthapuram

Khadi and Village Industries Commission KVIC): It is a statutory body formed in April 1957 (During 2nd Five Year plan) (as per an RTI) by the Government of India, under the Act of Parliament, 'Khadi and Village Industries Commission Act of 1956'. It is an apex organisation under the Ministry of Micro, Small and Medium Enterprises, with regard to khadi and village industries within India
In April 1957, it took over the work of former All India Khadi and Village Industries Board. Its head office is in Mumbai

Agricultural and Processed Food Products Export Development Authority (APEDA): APEDA is an Indian Apex-Export Trade Promotion Active government body.
It was set up by the Ministry of Commerce and Industry under the Agriculture and Processed Food products Export Development Authority. The Act was passed by Parliament in December 1985. It was formed and came into effect from 13 February 1986 by the notification issued in the Gazette of India. Headquarters: New Delhi. It is the premier body of export promotion of fresh vegetables and fruits. It provides the crucial interface between farmers, storehouses, packers, exporters, surface transport, ports, Railways, Airways, and all others engaged in export trade to the international market

National Agricultural Cooperative Marketing Federation of India (NAFED): It was established on the auspicious day of Gandhi Jayanti on 2nd October 1958.

Headquarters: New Delhi, India
Nafed was set up with the object to promote Co-operative marketing of agricultural produce to benefit the farmers.

Tribal Cooperative Marketing Federation of India (TRIFED): It is a national level cooperative body under the administrative control of Ministry of Tribal Affairs. It was established in 1987 and became operational in 1988. Headquarters: New Delhi. It was established under the Multi-state co-operative societies act 1984 under the former Ministry of Welfare.
Later it came under the control of Ministry of Tribal affairs.
It was formed with the main objective of institutionalizing the trade of Minor Forest products (MFP) and to provide the tribals of India a fair price for the surplus agricultural products produced by them.

Food Corporation of India (FCI): It is under the ownership of Ministry of Consumer Affairs, Food and Public Distribution, Government of India formed by the enactment of Food Corporation Act, 1964. The Food Corporation of India or the FCI was set up on 14 January 1965, with its initial headquarters at Chennai. Later this was moved to New Delhi. Its top official is designated as Chairman who is a civil servant of the IAS cadre

Indian Farmers Fertilizer Cooperative Limited (IFFCO): IFFCO was conceived and registered on 3 November 1967, as a multi-unit cooperative society with the primary objective of production and distribution of fertilizers. It is headquartered in New Delhi.

Institute of Chartered Accountants of India (ICAI): It is the national professional accounting body of India under the jurisdiction of Ministry of Corporate Affairs. It was established on 1 July 1949 as a statutory body under the Chartered Accountants Act, 1949 enacted by the Parliament (acting as the provisional Parliament of India) to regulate the profession in India. HOs - New Delhi
ICAI is solely responsible and accountable for setting the Standards on Auditing (SAs) to be followed in the audit of financial statements in India.

Federation of Indian Chambers of Commerce & Industry (FICCI): It is a non-governmental trade association and advocacy group based in India.

It was established in 1927, on the advice of Mahatma Gandhi by GD Birla and Purshottamdas Thakurdas, it is the largest, oldest and the apex business organization in India. It is headquartered in the national capital New Delhi and has a presence in 12 states in India and 8 countries across the world.
FICCI Ladies Organisation was established in 1983 to promote entrepreneurship and professional excellence among women in
India

India Meteorological Department (IMD): It is an agency of the Ministry of Earth Sciences of the Government of India. India Meteorology Department was established in 1875.
IMD is headquartered in Delhi and operates hundreds of observation stations across India and Antarctica. Regional offices are at Chennai, Mumbai, Kolkata, Nagpur, Guwahati and New Delhi. IMD became a member of the World Meteorological Organisation after independence on 27 April 1949.

National Green Tribunal (NGT): The National Green Tribunal was established on 18.10.2010 under the National Green Tribunal Act 2010. For effective and expeditious disposal of cases relating to environmental protection and conservation of forests and other natural resources. The Principal Bench of the NGT is in New Delhi.
The Chairperson of the NGT is a retired Judge of the Supreme Court, headquartered in New Delhi. On 18 October 2010, Justice Lokeshwar Singh Panta became its first Chairman.

National Highways Authority of India (NHAI): National Highways Authority of India was set up by an act of the Parliament, NHAI Act, 1988. It is a nodal agency of the Ministry of Road Transport and Highways.

On 10 February 1995, NHAI came into operations and was formally made an autonomous body

HQs - New Delhi

Yogendra Narain was the first Chairman of NHAI in 1988.

Association of Mutual Funds of India (AMFI): It is an industry standards organization in India in the mutual funds sector

The organization aims to develop the mutual funds market in India, by improving ethical and professional standards. AMFI was incorporated on 22 August 1995.

HQs - Mumbai

Advertising Standards Council of India (ASCI): It was established in 1985, is a self-regulatory voluntary organization of the advertising industry in India. HQs - Mumbai

Gem and Jewellery Export Promotion Council (GJEPC): It is an organization set up by the Government of India (GOI) with aim to promote the Indian gem and jewellery industry and its products. The GJEPC was established in 1966 by the Ministry of Commerce and Industry.

It has its headquarter in Mumbai.

GJEPC was granted autonomous status in 1998.

Export Credit Guarantee Corporation of India (ECGC): It provides export credit insurance support to Indian exporters and is controlled by the Ministry of Commerce and Industry, Government of India. Government of India had initially set up Export Risks Insurance Corporation (ERIC) in July 1957.

It was transformed into Export Credit and Guarantee Corporation Limited (ECGC) in 1964 and to Export Credit Guarantee Corporation of India in 1983. It is based in Mumbai

Archaeological Survey of India (ASI): It is attached to the Ministry of Culture that is responsible for archaeological research and the conservation and preservation of cultural monuments in the country. ASI was founded in 1861 by Alexander Cunningham who also became its first Director-General. HQs - New Delhi

The ASI is headed by a Director General who is assisted by an Additional Director General, two Joint Directors General, and 17 Directors

Spices Board of India: The Spices Board is the Indian government regulatory and export promotion agency for Indian spices. The Spices Board was constituted in 1987 under Spices Board Act 1986 with the responsibility of production/development of cardamom and export promotion of 52 spices shown in the schedule of the Act. The board is headquartered in Kochi

LIST OF SCHEMES AS PER BUDGET 2024.

1. Viksit Bharat by 2047: The government proposed a 50-year interest-free loan of Rs.75,000 crore to support the milestone-linked reforms by the State Governments, which will help to achieve Viksit Bharat 2047 goal.

2. Rooftop Solarisation Scheme: PM Suryodaya Yojana, which aims to achieve 300 units of free electricity per month to one crore households through rooftop solarisation.

3. Cervical Cancer Vaccination: In the Budget 2024, the government proposed to encourage vaccination for girls in the age group between 9 to 14 years for the prevention of cervical cancer.

4. Atmanirbhar Oil Seeds Abhiyan: The government will formulate a strategy to achieve 'Atmanirbharta' for oil seeds, such as groundnut, mustard, soybean, sesame and sunflower. This scheme, or Abhiyan, will cover the widespread adoption of modern farming techniques, research for high-yielding varieties, value addition, procurement, market linkages and crop insurance.

5. Dairy Development: The government will formulate a comprehensive programme for supporting dairy farmers. The programme will control foot and mouth disease. It will be built based on the success of the existing schemes, such as the National Livestock Mission, Rashtriya Gokul Mission and Infrastructure Development Funds for Dairy Processing and Animal Husbandry.

6. Corpus for Research and Innovation: The government will set up a Rs.1 lakh crore corpus with a 50-year interest-free loan. This corpus will provide long-term financing or refinancing with long tenors and nil or low-interest rates to encourage the private sector to scale up innovation and research in sunrise domains significantly.

7. Scheme for Bio-Manufacturing and Bio-Foundry: The government will launch a new scheme of bio-manufacturing and bio-foundry to promote green growth. This scheme will provide environmentally friendly alternatives, such as bioplastics, biodegradable polymers, bio-agri-inputs and biopharmaceuticals. It will also help transform today's consumptive manufacturing paradigm into regenerative principles.

8. Blue Economy 2.0: The government will launch a scheme for adaptation and restoration measures, coastal aquaculture and mariculture with an integrated and multi-sectorial approach to promote climate-resilient activities for blue economy 2.0.

9. PM Awas Yojana (Grameen): The government plans to provide two crore more houses in the next five years to meet the requirements arising from the increase in families under the PM Awas Yojana (Grameen). The government is close to achieving the two crore house target under this scheme despite the challenges due to COVID-19.

10. Maternal and Child Health Care: The government will bring various maternal and childcare schemes under one comprehensive programme to boost its implementation. There will be an expedition in the upgradation of Anganwadi centres under the 'Saksham Anganwadi and Poshan 2.0' for early childhood care, improved nutrition delivery and development. The government will also roll out the newly designed U-WIN platform for managing immunisation and expeditiously intensifying efforts of the 'Mission Indradhanush' throughout the country.

11. Ayushman Bharat: Healthcare cover under the Ayushman Bharat scheme will be extended to all Anganwadi workers, helpers, and ASHA workers.

12. Nano DAP: The application of Nano DAP on various crops will be extended after the successful adoption of Nano Urea on various crops in all agro-climatic zones.

13. PM Matsya Sampada Yojana: The establishment of the Department for Fisheries has resulted in a doubling of inland and aquaculture production and seafood export.

The government will implement the following under the Pradhan Mantri Matsya Sampada Yojana (PMMSY): Enhance aquaculture productivity from the existing 3 tons to 5 tons per hectare, Double exports to Rs.1 lakh crore
Generate 55 lakh employment opportunities in the near future, Set up five integrated aquaparks

14. Lakhpati Didi: The government has enhanced the target for Lakhpati Didi from two crore to three crore based on the success of nearly one crore women. Eighty-three lakh Self Help Groups (SHGs) with nine crore women are transforming the rural socio-economic landscape with self-reliance and empowerment, due to which nearly one crore women have become Lakhpati Didi.

Achievements of Existing Government Schemes

1. Pradhan Mantri Gareeb Kalyan Yojana: There has been a Direct Benefit Transfer (DBT) of Rs 34 lakh crore from the government using the PM Jan Dhan accounts, leading to savings of Rs 2.7 lakh crore for the government. The savings have helped to provide more funds for 'Garib Kalyan'.

2. PM-SVANidhi: PM-SVANidhi Yojana has provided credit assistance to 78 lakh street vendors. Out of this, a total of 2.3 lakh vendors have received credit for the third time.

3. PM-KISAN Yojana: Under Pradhan Mantri Kisan Samman Nidhi (PM-KISAN) Yojana, direct financial assistance is provided to 11.8 crore farmers every year, including al and small farmers.

4. PM Fasal Bima Yojana (PMFBY): The government has provided crop insurance to four crore farmers under the PM Fasal Bima Yojana (PMFBY).

5. Skill India Mission: The Skill India Mission has reskilled and upskilled 54 lakh youth, trained 1.4 crore youth and established 3,000 new ITIs. Many new institutions of higher learning, including 15 AIIMS, 7 IITs, 7 IIMs, 16 IIITs and 390 universities, have been set up.

6. PM Mudra Yojana: There has been a sanction of 43 crore loans for the entrepreneurial aspirations of our youth under the PM Mudra Yojana, aggregating to Rs.22.5 lakh crore. There has been a sanction of 30 crore PM Mudra Yojana loans to women entrepreneurs.

7. PM Awas Yojana: Under the PM Awas Yojana (Rural), over 70% of houses are given to women as joint or sole owners, which has enhanced their dignity.

8. Pradhan Mantri Kisan Sampada Yojana: The implementation of the Pradhan Mantri Kisan Sampada Yojana has provided benefits to 38 lakh farmers and generated 10 lakh employment.

9. Pradhan Mantri Formalisation of Micro Food Processing Enterprises Yojana: With the implementation of the Pradhan Mantri Formalisation of Micro Food Processing Enterprises (PMFME) Yojana, there has been assistance to 2.4 lakh SHGs and 60,000 individuals with credit linkages.

ON-GOING SCHEMES:

1. PMJDY (Pradhan Mantri Jan Dhan Yojana): August 28, 2014, Ministry of Finance

2. PMSSY (Pradhan Mantri Swasthya Suraksha Yojana): January 22, 2015, Ministry of Health & Family Welfare

3. PMSSY (Pradhan Mantri Swasthya Suraksha Yojana): January 22, 2015, Ministry of Health & Family Welfare

4. PMMY (Pradhan Mantri Mudra Yojana): April 8, 2015, Ministry of Finance

5. PMJJBY (Pradhan Mantri Jeevan Jyoti Bima Yojana): May 9, 2015, Ministry of Finance

6. PMSBY (Pradhan Mantri Suraksha Bima Yojana): May 9, 2015, Ministry of Finance

7. APY (Atal Pension Yojana): May 9, 2015 Ministry of Finance

8. KVP (Kisan Vikas Patra): 2014, Ministry of Finance

9. GMS (Gold Monetisation Scheme): November 4, 2015, Ministry of Finance

10. PMFBY (Pradhan Mantri Fasal Bima Yojana): February 18, 2016, Ministry of Agriculture

11. PMGKY (Pradhan Mantri Krishi Sinchai Yojana): July 1, 2015, Ministry of Agriculture

12. DDUGJY (Deen Dayal Upadhyaya Gram Jyoti Yojana): July 25, 2015, Ministry of Power

13. RGM (Rashtriya Gokul Mission): December 16, 2014, Ministry of Agriculture and Farmers Welfare

14. Digital India: July 1, 2015, Ministry of Electronics and Information Technology

15. Skill India: July 15, 2015, Ministry of Skill Development and Entrepreneurs

16. (PMKVY) Pradhan Mantri Kaushal Vikas Yojana: 2015, Ministry of Skill Development and Entrepreneurs

17. Make in India: September 25, 2014, Ministry of Commerce and Industry

18. Startup India, Standup India: January 16, 2016, Government of India

19. Pradhan Mantri Garib Kalyan Yojana (PMGKY): December 16, 2016

20. Swachh Bharat Abhiyan: October 2nd, 2014, Ministry of Housing and Urban Affairs

21. Pradhan Mantri Bhartiya Janaushadhi Pariyojana' (PMBJP) (PMJAY): Septembe r 2015, Ministry of Chemicals and Fertilizers

22. National Digital Health Mission (NDHM): August 15, 2020, Ministry of Health and Family Welfare

23. BBBPY (Beti Bachao, Beti Padhao Yojana): January 22, 2015, Ministry of Women and Child Development

24. Namami Gange: June 2014, Ministry of Water Resources

Schemes in details:
1. Pradhan Mantri MUDRA Yojana (PMMY): Pradhan Mantri Mudra Yojana (PMMY) is a flagship scheme of the Government of India launched on April 8, 2015, that provides collateral-free loans ranging from ₹50,000 to ₹20 lakh to non-corporate, non-farm small/micro enterprises. It aims to empower new

entrepreneurs and provide financial support to small businesses. Provides loans up to ₹10 lakh for micro/small non-corporate, non-farm enterprises, categorized as Shishu (up to ₹50,000), Kishor (up to ₹5 lakh), and Tarun (up to ₹10 lakh).

2. Startup India Seed Fund Scheme (SISFS): The Startup India Seed Fund Scheme (SISFS) provides financial assistance up to ₹50 Lakhs (convertible debt/debt) and ₹20 Lakhs (grant) to eligible early-stage startups for proof of concept, prototypes, trials, and market entry. Launched with ₹945 Crore, it supports startups through recognized incubators, aiming to bridge the early-stage funding gap. The Startup India Seed Fund Scheme (SISFS) was officially launched on April 19, 2021, by the Union Minister for Commerce and Industry, Piyush Goyal. It offers financial assistance for proof of concept, prototype development, and market entry, with grants up to ₹20 lakh and debt funding up to ₹50 lakh per startup.

3. Credit Guarantee Scheme for Startups (CGSS): The Credit Guarantee Scheme for Startups (CGSS), launched by the DPIIT in 2022, provides collateral-free, debt-based funding up to ₹20 crore per borrower to eligible DPIIT-recognized startups. It supports Member Lending Institutions (MLIs) in offering loans, including venture debt and working capital, with guarantee coverage of up to 85% for loans up to ₹10 crore, aiding in easier access to credit. It Provides up to ₹5 crore in credit guarantees for eligible startups, ensuring financial support without requiring collateral.

4. The Credit Guarantee Fund Trust for Micro and Small Enterprises (CGTMSE) scheme provides collateral-free loans up to ₹5 crore (effective April 1, 2023) to new and existing MSMEs. Jointly launched by the Government of India and SIDBI, it guarantees 75% to 80% of the loan amount in case of default. The Credit Guarantee Trust Fund for Micro and Small Enterprises (CGTMSE) was officially launched on August 30, 2000, and became operational effective from January 1, 2000. It was established by the Government of India and SIDBI to provide collateral-free credit to MSMEs.

Key Features of the CGTMSE Scheme
Collateral-Free: No collateral or third-party guarantee required for loans up to ₹5 Crore.
Guarantee Coverage: Generally covers 75% to 85% of the sanctioned loan amount, depending on the borrower profile and loan size.
Maximum Loan Limit: Up to ₹5 crore for eligible MSMEs.
Eligible Borrowers: New and existing micro and small enterprises (including service and manufacturing sectors).
Lending Institutions: Available through banks and NBFCs registered as Member Lending Institutions (MLIs) of CGTMSE.

Eligibility Criteria
Entity Type: Manufacturing and service enterprises (micro and small).
Exclusions: Educational institutions, agriculture, training institutes, and SHGs are generally not eligible.
Track Record: Borrower must have a good credit history and should not be a defaulter with any financial institution.

5. Atal Innovation Mission (AIM): The Atal Innovation Mission (AIM), under NITI Aayog, aims to cultivate a comprehensive culture of innovation and entrepreneurship across India. Established in 2016, its key objectives are to develop new programs and policies that promote creativity, provide mentoring for startups, and foster a problem-solving mindset in schools and industries.

Core Pillars and Key Programs:
Atal Tinkering Labs (ATLs): Set up in schools (grades 6-12) to foster creativity and technological skills through tools like 3D printing.

Atal Incubation Centres (AICs): Nurture startups in technology-driven sectors, providing infrastructure, mentoring, and funding.
Atal Community Innovation Centres (ACICs): Focus on encouraging innovation in underserved regions of the country.
Atal New India Challenges (ANIC): Address societal and industrial problems through innovation in key sectors.
Mentor of Change Program: A national network of experts providing pro-bono mentoring to students and innovators.

Key Goals and Impact:
1. Promotion of Entrepreneurship: Nurturing start-up businesses to become scalable and sustainable enterprises.
2. Innovation Ecosystem: Creating an umbrella structure that oversees the innovation landscape across universities, industries, and NGOs.
3. Collaborative Platforms: Building partnerships between government, academia, and industry to foster sustainable innovation.

AIM has established over 10,000 Atal Tinkering Labs and supported thousands of startups and innovators across the country.
It offers grants up to ₹10 crore for innovative projects and startups.

6. MSME Creative Component Scheme (IC Scheme): The MSME Creative Component Scheme is formally known as the Design Component under the broader MSME Innovative Scheme (formerly CLCS-TUS), launched by the Ministry of Micro, Small & Medium Enterprises, Government of India. The MSME Innovative Scheme—which combines the incubation, design, and IPR components—was launched on March 10, 2022. This scheme aims to bring Indian manufacturing MSMEs and design experts onto a common platform, providing expert advice and cost-effective solutions for new product development and improvement.

Key Components and Assistance:
The scheme includes Design Projects (expert consultancy) and Design Awareness Programs (seminars/workshops).

Financial Support: The GoI supports approved projects with grants for design strategies, detailing, and prototyping.
Grant Structure:
Design Projects: 75% for Micro, 60% for Small/Medium, up to ₹40 lakh.
Student Projects: 75% of costs up to ₹2.5 lakh.
It offers up to 95% of airfare and space rent for entrepreneurs participating in exhibitions.

7. Credit Linked Capital Subsidy Scheme (CLCSS): The Credit Linked Capital Subsidy Scheme (CLCSS), often referred to as the Technology Upgradation Scheme, is a Government of India initiative providing a 15% upfront capital subsidy (up to ₹15 lakh) to Micro and Small Enterprises (MSEs) for upgrading technology with modern plant and machinery. It promotes modernization, improved quality, and increased productivity in manufacturing sectors. The Credit Linked Capital Subsidy Scheme (CLCSS) was officially launched on October 1, 2000. The scheme enables 15% subsidies (up to ₹15 lakh) for technology upgrades in small-scale manufacturing.

8. Stand Up India Scheme: The Stand-Up India scheme was launched by Prime Minister Narendra Modi on April 5, 2016, to facilitate bank loans between ₹10 lakh and ₹1 crore to at least one SC/ST borrower and one woman borrower per bank branch for setting up greenfield enterprises. The scheme focuses on providing loans between ₹10 lakh and ₹1 crore to SC/ST and women entrepreneurs for greenfield enterprises.

Financial Schemes of Northeast
Northeastern Development Finance Corporation Ltd (NEDFL) Schemes
Related scheme

i) Corporate Finance:

Description: Providing finance such as normal capital expenditure, working capital margin, short fall in working capital, repayment of high-cost debt and general corporate purpose like funding of business acquisition or for brand building, etc., where no tangible asset creation may be envisaged.

Nature of assistance: Minimum exposure would be Rs.50 lakh and maximum exposure shall be as per exposure norms.

Who can apply: Corporates with minimum 3 years of profitable operations for NEDFi assisted units, in case of other units the unit should have minimum 5 years of operations.

ii) Equipment Finance:

Description: This scheme intends to provide financial assistance for acquiring specific machinery/ equipment by financially sound and profit-making companies having good credit record. The proposed unit should be located in any of the eight North Eastern States.

Nature of assistance: Composite loan comprising term loan and working capital; maximum project size should be Rs.25 lakh term loan from NEDFi, maximum up to 75% of the project cost, promoter's contribution will be 25% of the project cost.

Who can apply: Graduates and Postgraduates in agriculture and allied subjects. Graduates, post-graduates from other disciplines having experience and skill to undertake Agri Business ventures can also be considered. The proposed units could be proprietorship, partnership or a company. The promoter or their units must not be a defaulter in any government scheme and /or with any bank or any other agencies. The proposed unit for which financial assistance is sought should be located within any of the eight North-Eastern States.

iii) Micro Finance:

Description: The scheme envisages meeting micro credit needs small and medium size agriculturists, self-employed personnel and entrepreneurs can be reached much more effectively by involving the services of intermediaries, who can understand needs, demand and local situations. Developing and supporting NGOs/ Voluntary Agencies (VAs) with good track record for on-lending to the "needy" for taking up any income generating activities in the rural areas.

Nature of assistance: NEDFi would lend the amount at Prime Lending Rate (PLR) + 0.5 % (administrative charge). Processing fee to the extent of maximum 1% of loan amount. The MFI have to comply with RBI norms. Repayment period is maximum 5 years.

Who can apply: All MFIs which have been in existence for at least 3 years; the MFIs should have good credibility record. Voluntary agencies are also eligible to apply.

iv) NEDFi Equity Fund:

Description: The schemes intends to invest in projects promoted by entrepreneurs in North-Eastern Region having sound business ideas with potential for high growth and more than normal returns on investment.

Nature of assistance: Investment in a single project would range from Rs.50-300 lakhs. Assistance will be available for financing terms normally included in the cost of a project, startup working capital and selectively for core current assets during commercial operation.

Who can apply: Individual entrepreneurs or groups of entrepreneurs; The applicant should have a viable business plan which offers above average profitability leading to attractive returns on investment.

v) NEDFi Opportunity Scheme for Small Enterprises (NoSSE):

Description: The scheme aims at providing long term financial assistance for setting up new industrial and infrastructure projects as well as for expansion, diversification or modernization of existing industrial enterprises, excluding commercial real estates.

Nature of assistance: If the project cost is above Rs.50 lakhs and up to Rs 200 lakhs loan component up to a maximum of Rs 100 lakhs in the form of term loan or working capital or combination of both.

Who can apply: Local small entrepreneurs of Northeast India.

vi) Northeast Entrepreneur Development (NEED):

Description The scheme has been formulated to help first generation entrepreneurs who are short of equity. New projects in Micro and Small Enterprises, expansion, modernization of existing units. Technical qualifications of the promoter in the relevant field is a pre-requisite.

Nature of assistance: Term loan up to a maximum of 75% of the project cost including one cycle of working capital in deserving cases. Promoter's contribution minimum 25% of project cost.

Who can apply: First generation entrepreneurs, existing entrepreneurs, proprietary & partnership concerns and companies.

LIST OF IMPORTANT COMMITTEES:

1. Arun Goel Committee: To strengthen the Capital Goods (CG) Sector.

2. P K Mohanty Committee: To review present ownership guidelines and corporate structure for Indian Private Sector Banks.

3. One Man Committee to Prevent Stubble burning in Punjab, Haryana, and Uttar Pradesh which is a source of pollution in the Delhi-national capital region (NCR): headed by Justice Madan B. Lokur

4. Rajiv Mehrishi Committee: To measure the impact on the national economy and financial stability of waiving of interest and COVID-19 related moratorium.

5. KV Kamath Committee: Setting parameters for Loan Restructuring

6. Pradip Shah Committee: To develop international retail business at the International Financial Services Centre (IFSC)

7. Abid Hussain Committee: Small scale industries and Trade Policy Reform

8. Chakravarty Committee (1985): Monetary policy

9. G V Ramakrishna Committee: Disinvestment

10. Raja Chelliah Committee: Tax reforms in India

11. Khusro Committee: Agricultural Credit System

12. Sarkaria Commission: Relationship and power balance between the Centre and States

13. Malegam Committee: Microfinance

14. Narasimhan Committee: Banking Reforms

Foreign Direct Investment (FDI) was allowed in insurance upto 26% wherein the foreign players were allowed to enter into joint ventures with domestic players

Lot of domestic players joined hands with foreign partners who brought in valuable expertise and capital.

Opening up of the insurance sector has led to emergence of innovative insurance products and has also helped in deeper spread of insurance.

Liberalization brought in the much-needed competition and better customer service.

Insurance Regulatory Development Authority of India (IRDAI): - The IRDAI is an independent and autonomous statutory body. IRDAI was constituted under the Insurance Regulatory and Development Authority Act which was passed in 1999. The main function of the IRDAI is to regulate the insurance industry of the country.

For many years the insurance sector of India was protected. The IRDA Act of 1999 allowed the entry of private companies in the insurance sector. It also allowed for 26% investment by foreign companies. Since 2014 the FDI limit has been increased to 49% and further opened up the insurance sector.

So, the Insurance Regulatory and Development Authority of India has a role to protect the policyholders from any form of discriminatory practices. They regulate all the insurance companies. All companies have to approach the IRDAI for registration certificates. And they are responsible for the renewal, modification or cancellation of these certificates.

Functions and Powers of the IRDAI: The IRDA Act gives the authority its functions and powers. Section 14 of the Act contains the scope of powers of the Insurance Regulatory and Development Authority of India to regulate the insurance and reinsurance industry. Let us take a look at the powers and functions of the IRDAI. The IRDAI has the authority to issue registration certificates to any applicant. The also may re-issue, renew, cancel or modify these certificates as per their discretion.

a) Protection of the policyholders in matters such as assigning of policy, nominating members to the policy, insurable interest, settlement of claims, and any other such matters.

b) Make guidelines and provide training for the appropriate code of conduct for insurance agents and intermediaries

c) Also making the code of conduct for loss assessors and surveyors working with the insurance companies.

d) They can also conduct investigations and audits of insurance companies, intermediaries, and any other organizations with a connection to the insurance business.

e) The IRDAI can also dictate the manner in which the insurance companies have to maintain their records and books of accounts. And how they prepare their final accounts as well.

f) They regulate how the insurance companies invest their funds and maintain their margin of solvency.

g) The adjudication of matters and disputes of any kind involving the insurance companies or intermediaries is also done by the IRDAI

h) There is a Tariff Advisory Committee with relation to the insurance company. The IRDAI regulates its functions as well.

Role of IRDAI as a Business Facilitator: One function of the Insurance Regulatory and Development Authority of India is that it also acts as a business facilitator. It regulates the insurance industry and creates trust and goodwill in the market for these insurance companies.

The IRDAI is also responsible for the growth and development of the insurance sector. The increasing participation of foreign companies under the watchful eye of the authorities is good for both the insurance sector and the economy as a whole.

Different Types of Insurance:
a) Life Insurance
b) General Insurance: - Fire Insurance, Marine Insurance, Miscellaneous (Motor, Liability, Health, Burglary)

Life Insurance: Life insurance deals with covering the lives of human beings. In life insurance, the asset in question is the 'economic value' of the person. A person's earning capacity depends on his skills, knowledge, ability and other factors. The family, employer and indirectly the users of products created by this asset (human beings) enjoy value and benefits. A human life is an income generating asset. But this asset can be lost through unexpected, early death or made non-functional through illnesses or disabilities caused by accidents. Death is certain, but its timing is uncertain. If death occurs very early in the career, insurance contributes to help those dependent on this asset.

General Insurance: Non-life insurance or general insurance deals with covering non-human objects like animals, agricultural crops, goods, factories, cars etc. In some countries nonlife insurance is also known as Property and Casualty Insurance. Non-life insurance also covers losses through individual behaviors like fraud, burglary, non-fulfilment of promises (in the case of repayment of mortgage loans) and negligence by professionals in their service. General insurance policies are mostly for one year and are renewable.

Fire insurance deals with all fire related risks and will include damage due to riots, malicious acts, typhoons, cyclones, earthquakes and consequential expenditures related to these events.

Marine insurance deals with goods being transported by sea, air, rail or road as well as all marine related risks.

Apart from fire insurance and marine insurance all other businesses are included in the miscellaneous class. These include motor insurance, engineering, liability, burglary, fidelity, health, personal accident etc.

Accidents and illnesses to human beings are covered in health (non-life) insurance in India. But these are covered in life insurance in many countries. In India accidents and some critical illnesses are covered in life insurance only as additional cover (riders) along with the main life insurance policy. In India, insurance on life of a person for death by accident only is treated as non- life insurance.

Principles of Insurance: -
Utmost Good faith
Insurable Interest
Principle of Indemnity
Principle of Contribution
Principle of Subrogation
Principle of Loss Minimization
Principle of 'Causa Proxima'

Types of Insurance Plans: -

Endowment Insurance Plan: Endowment plan is a life insurance policy which provides you with a combination of both i.e. an insurance cover, as well as savings plan. It is an insurance cum investment plan that offers maturity benefits in addition to death benefits.

Group Life Insurance Plan: A Group life insurance plan provides coverage to members of a group that tends to be employees of a company or members of an organization. Members of the group usually receive insurance at a reduced cost because the insurer's risk is spread across a group of policyholders.

Micro Insurance Plan: Micro Insurance is a mechanism to protect low income people against risk, such as accident, illness, and natural disasters, in exchange for insurance premium payments tailored to their needs, income and level of risk.

Joint Life Insurance Plan: Joint Life Insurance Plan is a life insurance policy that covers multiple people. Most joint life insurance

Single Life Insurance Plan: A Single Life Insurance Policy covers one person only and pays out the chosen amount of cover if that person dies during the length of the policy.

Convertible Insurance Plan: Policy that allows an insured to cover whole life insurance without having to prove his or her insurability

Pure Endowment Plan: A Pure Endowment is a type of insurance in which an insurance company agrees to pay the insured a certain amount of money if the insured is still alive at the end of a specific period of time. There are, however, no beneficiaries to a pure endowment means that no benefits will be owed if the insured is not alive by the end of the endowment period.

Types of Insurance Policies: a) General Insurance Policy b) Life Insurance Policy

a) General Insurance Policies: - Home Insurance Policies, Renter's Insurance Policies, Medical or Health Insurance Policies, Pets Insurance Policies, Travel Insurance Policies, Business Insurance Policies

Home Insurance: As the name suggests, a home insurance policy protect your home and its belongings from the damages suffered due to manmade or natural disasters. One can obtain cover against the risk of loss to residence and property

Renter's insurance: A Renter's insurance policy is a group of coverages designed to help protect you and your belongings. A typical renter's insurance policy includes liability coverage, protection for your belongings and coverage for additional expenses, should the home you are renting become temporarily inhabitable.

Health Insurance: An essential risk mitigating tool, health insurance prevents out-of-pocket expenses while dealing with a medical emergency. A general health insurance plan is an indemnity plan that pays for hospitalization expenses up to the sum insured. While you can avail of a standalone health policy, family floater plans provide coverage to all the members of your family. On the other hand, critical illness plans are fixed-benefit plans which provide a lump sum upon diagnosis of a critical ailment, taking care of pre- and post-hospitalisation costs. These plans help take care of astronomical costs associated with the treatment of critical ailments.

Pets Insurance: Pet Insurance policy is one of the latest insurance schemes introduced in India. This scheme covers veterinary expenses incurred for the treatment of a pet who has endured an injury or is sick. Some pet insurance plans also cover death or loss of the pet that is insured.

Travel Insurance: In case you are traveling abroad, a travel insurance policy protects you against losses suffered due to loss of baggage, delays in flight and trip cancellation. In some cases, if you are hospitalized while traveling, travel insurance may also offer cashless hospitalization.

Business Insurance: Business Insurance Policy protects businesses from losses due to events that may occur during the normal course of business. There are many types of business insurance including coverage for property damage, legal liability and employee related risks.

Life Insurance Policies:
a) Term Insurance Policies
b) Money Back Insurance Policies
c) Whole Life Policies
d) Unit Link Investment Policies
e) Pension Policies

Term Insurance: It is a form of life cover, it provides coverage for a defined period of time, and if the insured expires during the term of the policy then death benefit is payable to the nominee. Term plans are specifically designed to secure your family needs in case of death or uncertainty. It provides a specific amount of coverage for a specific period of time.

Money Back Insurance: In Money Back Insurance the insured person gets a percentage of sum assured at regular interval, instead of getting the lump sum amount at the end of the term. It is an endowment plan with the benefit of liquidity.

Whole Life Insurance Plan: Whole life Insurance is a contract that provides insurance coverage of the contract holders for his or her entire life. Upon the inevitable death of the contract holder, the insurance payout is made to the contract's beneficiaries. These policies also include a savings component, which accumulates a cash value. This cash value is one of the key elements of whole life insurance.

Unit Link Investment Policy: Unit Linked Insurance Plan is a market linked product that aggregates the very best of investment and insurance. It is a plan linked to capital market and offers flexibility to invest in equity or debt funds as per risk appetite.

Pension Policy: A pension plan is the retirement amount which an individual gets from their insurance companies on a regular basis or in the form of a lump sum.

The Insurance Ombudsman: The Central Government under the powers of the Insurance Act, 1938 made Redressal of Public Grievances Rules, 1998 by a notification published in the official gazette on November 11, 1998. These rules apply to life and non- life insurance, for all personal lines of insurance, that is, insurances taken in an individual capacity.
b) The objective of these rules is to resolve all complaints relating to settlement of claims on the part of the insurance companies in a cost effective, efficient and impartial manner.
c) The Ombudsman, by the mutual agreement of the insured and the insurer can act as a mediator and counselor within the terms of insurance.
d) At present there are 17 Insurance Ombudsman in different locations.
e) The decision of the Ombudsman, whether to accept or reject the complaint is final.

Complaint to the Ombudsman: Any complaint made to the Ombudsman should be in writing, signed by the insured or his legal heirs, addressed to the ombudsman within whose jurisdiction, the insurer has a branch / office, supported by documents, if any, along with an estimate of the nature and extent of loss to the complainant and the relief sought.

Complaints can be made to the Ombudsman if: The complainant had made a previous written representation to the insurance company and the insurance company had:
a) Rejected the Complaint or
b) The Complainant had not received any reply within one month after receipt of the complaint by the insurer
c) The Complainant is not satisfied with the reply given by the insurer.

1) The complaint is made within one year from the date of rejection by the insurance company.
2) The complaint is not pending in any Court or Consumer Forum or in arbitration.
3) Any dispute about premium paid or payable in terms of insurance policy.
4) Any partial or total repudiation of claims by the Life insurer, General insurer or the Health insurer.

Recommendation by the Ombudsman:
1) A copy of the acceptance letter by the insured should be sent to the insurer and his written confirmation sought within 15 days of his receiving such acceptance letter.

2) If the dispute is not settled by intermediation, the Ombudsman will pass an award to the insured which he thinks is fair, and is not more than what is necessary to cover the loss of the insured.

3) Recommendations should be made within one month of the receipt of such a complaint.

4) The copies should be sent to both the complaint and the insurance company.

5) Recommendations have to be accepted in writing by the complainant within 15 days of receipt of such recommendations.

Awards by the Ombudsman

The awards by the Ombudsman are governed by the following rules:

a) The award should not be more than 20 lakh (inclusive of ex-gratia payment and other expenses).

b) The award should be made within a period of 3 months from the date of receipt of such a complaint, and the insured should acknowledge the receipt of the award in full as a final settlement within one month of such award.

c) The insurer shall comply with the award and send a written intimation to the Ombudsman within 15 days of the receipt of such acceptance letter.

d) If the insured does not intimate in writing the acceptance of such an award, the insurer may not implement the award.

Schemes Related to Insurance

1) Atal Pension Yojana: Pension Between Rs. 1000 and Rs. 5000 a month. All individuals between 18 and 40, who will have to contribute till they turn 60.

2) Pradhan Mantri Suraksha Bima Yojana: Accidental death and disability cover of Rs 2 lakh, Premium is Rs 12 per year, anybody who has a savings account in the banks that offer this scheme.

3) Pradhan Mantri Jeevan Jyoti Bima Yojana: A pure protection term insurance cover which pays Rs 2 lakh to dependents in the event of the policyholder's death. Premium is Rs 330 a year. Anybody in the age band of 18 - 70 years who has a savings account in a bank that offers this scheme.

4) Rashtriya Swasthya Bima Yojana: Hospitalisation cover upto Rs 30000 for a family of five on a floater basis. The beneficiary who is Below Poverty Line is eligible.

5) Pradhan Mantri Fasal Bima Yojana: The maximum premium payable by the farmers is 2% for all kharif food and oil seeds, 1.5% for Rabi food & oilseeds and 5% for annual commercial crops. Providing financial support to farmers suffering crop loss/ damage arising out of unforeseen events.

6) Employees State Insurance Corporation Scheme: Wage limit Rs 21,000. All employees of a covered unit, whose monthly income does not exceed Rs 21000 per month are eligible.

Insurance Terminologies

Actuary: A person with expertise in the fields of economics, statistics and mathematics, who helps in risk assessment and estimation of premiums etc for an insurance business

Actuarial Science: Actuarial science is the discipline that applies mathematical and statistical methods to assess risk in insurance, finance and other industries and professions.

Bancassurance: Bancassurance means selling insurance product through banks. Banks and insurance company come up in a partnership wherein the bank sells the tied insurance company's insurance products to its clients.

Third Party Administrator: It is an organization that processes insurance claims or certain aspects of employee benefit plans for a separate entity.

Mortality Charge: It is the amount charged every year by the insurer to provide the life cover to the policy holder on the life of life insured. It is also called the cost of insurance.

Maturity date: Maturity date refers to the date on which the principal and interest associated with a debt security must be repaid to the holder in its entirely.

Agent: An Agent is a person who represents an insurance firm and sells insurance policies on its behalf.

Broker: An Insurance Broker is someone who advises people on their insurance needs and negotiates insurance contracts on their behalf with insurers in return for a fee or commission.

Annuity: Annuity is a type of policy issued by an insurance company designed to accept and grow funds, and upon annuitization, create a stream of income or payments. The money you pay in can be either a lump sum or a number of payments.

Insurable Risk: A risk that confroms to the norms and specifications of the insurance policy in such a way that the criterion for insurance is fulfilled.

Lapse: The policy for which all benefits to the policy holder cease and is terminated due to non-payment of premium amount on the due date or even after the grace period.

Surrender value: It is the amount the policy holder will get from the life insurance company if he decides to exit the policy before maturity.

Maturity claim: The maturity claim amount is the payment received by the policy holder on paying the premium for the whole premium paying term and on completion of policy term.

Death claim: A death claim is a request to grant life insurance benefits due under the policy to the designated beneficiaries after the death of the insured.

Policy Not in Force: It means that the policy is paid up and active, so long as you are paying the premium for your life insurance your policy is considered "in force". If your policy is lapsed and you die, your insurer will not pay out on your policy.

Gratuity: Gratuity is a monetary benefit given by the employer to his employee at the time of retirement. It is a defined benefit plan where no contributions are made by the employee.

Void and Voidable contract: A contract will be considered Void when it requires one party to perform an act that is impossible or illegal. A Voidable contract is a void contract and can be enforced. Usually only one party is bound to the contract terms in a voidable contract.

Paid up value: Paid-up value is the reduced amount of sum assured paid by the insurance company, in case the policy holder discontinues payment of premiums. After payment of three years of premium in traditional life insurance plans, your policy automatically acquires paid up value.

Terminable Bonus: A bonus paid on a life insurance policy when the holder reaches a certain age or dies. Actual Cash Value: A valuation of the damaged property, i.e its monetary worth at market value immediately preceding the occurrence loss, is called actual cash value of the property. It gives the estimate of the cost of replacement or repair of the damaged asset.

Encumbrance: Encumbrance refer to claims to a property that is under the care, custody and control of another individual.

Liquidity: Liquidity means how quickly you can get your cash on your hands. In simpler terms, liquidity is to get your money whenever you need it.

Quick Liquidity Ratio: It is the total amount of a company's quick assets divided by the sum of its net liabilities and its reinsurance liabilities.

Current Liquidity: Current Liquidity is the total amount of cash and unaffiliated holdings compared with net liabilities and ceded reinsurance balances payable. Current Liquidity is expressed as a percentage, and is used to determine the amount of an insurance company's liabilities that can be covered with liquid assets.

Re insurance: It is a process whereby one entity (the insurer) takes on all or part of the risk covered under a policy issued by an insurance company in consideration of a premium payment. In other words, it is a form of insurance cover for insurance companies.

Lapse Ratio: It is the number of policies that are not renewed compared to the number of policies that were active at the beginning of that same period. The lapse ratio represents the percentage of policies that were not renewed and thus have lapsed in coverage.

Impaired Insure: An Impaired Insurer is an insurance company that is potentially unable to fulfill its policy obligations and has been placed under rehabilitation or conservation.

Dividend: Dividend refers to a reward, cash, or otherwise, that a company gives to its shareholders. Dividends can be issued in various forms, such as cash payment, stocks or any other form.

Co-insurance: Type of policy under which the insured must bear a fixed sum of loss in case of a claim

Coding Company: Coding is the process of translating a physician's documentation about a patient's medical condition and health services rendered into medical codes that are then plugged into a claim for processing with an insurance company.

Declaration: Part of a property or liability insurance policy that states the name and address of policy-holder, property insured, its location and description, the policy period, premiums, and supplemental information.

Casualty Insurance: Casualty insurance broadly encompasses insurance not directly concerned with life insurance, health insurance, or property insurance. Casualty insurance is mainly liability coverage of an individual or organization for negligent actions or omissions.

Retention: It refers to the amount of money an insured persons or business become responsible for in the event of a claim.

Fortuitous Loss: Loss occurring by accident or chance, not by anyone's intention. Insurance policies provide coverage against losses that occur only on a chance basis, where the insured cannot control the loss, thus the insured should not be able to burn down his or her own home and collect.

Indemnity: Indemnity means making compensation payments to one party by the other for the loss occurred.

Insured: Specifically named individual or firm with whom an insurance contract is made, and whose interests are protected under the policy. In some cases, more than one entity may be designated as insured.

Insurer: An insurer refers to the company providing you with financial coverage in the case of unexpected, bad events covered on your renters or homeowners policy.

Loss Reserve: Loss Reserve is an estimate of an insurer's liability from future claims. Loss reserves are typically comprised of liquid assets, and they allow the insurer to cover claims made against policy that it underwrites.

Pooling: It is a practice wherein a group of small firms join together to secure better insurance rates and coverage plans by virtue of their increased buying power as a block.

Premium: Premium is an amount paid periodically to the insurer by the insured for covering his risk.

Tort: A Tort is a wrongful action or omission that harms a person or business, prompting the injured party to seek compensation in civil court.

Waiver: The surrender of a right or privilege. In life insurance, a provision that sets certain conditions, such as disablement, which allow coverage to remain in force without payment of premiums.

Insured Peril: Specific source of loss (such as death, fire, liability) to cover which an insurance policy is issued

Blanket Bond: It refers to insurance coverage carried by banks and brokerage houses that protects against any losses incurred by unlawful or dishonest activity on the part of employees. It is also called blanket fidelity bond or fidelity bond.

Rider: A Rider is an insurance policy provision that adds benefits to or amends the terms of a basic insurance policy. Riders provide insured parties with options such as additional coverage , or they may even restrict or limit coverage.

Free lock Period: The free lock period is a required period of time in which a new life insurance policy owner can terminate the policy without penalties such as surrender charges.

Mortality Charge: It is the amount charged every year by the insurer to provide the life insurance cover to the policyholder on the life of the life insured.

Assured: A person who has been insured by some insurance company, or underwriter , against losses or perils mentioned in the policy of insurance.

Base Rate: The cost of a given unit of insurance for each specific type of auto coverage, such as bodily injury and property damage liability

Collusion: An agreement usually secret between two or more persons to defraud or deprive another or others of their property or rights

Grace Period: It is a defined amount of time after the premium is due in which a policy holder can make a premium payment without coverage lapsing.

Larceny: The unlawful taking of a person's personal property without his consent and with intent to deprive him of ownership or use. It is a broader term than burglary or robbery, largely synonymous with theft.

Deductible: A deductible is an amount of money subtracted from the value of a loss, which is not covered by insurance.

Umbrella Policy: An Umbrella insurance policy is extra liability insurance coverage that goes beyond the limits of the insured's home, auto or watercraft insurance.

ULIP- Unit Linked Insurance Plan: ULIP stands for unit linked insurance plans. ULIP is a combination of insurance and investment. Here policyholders can pay a premium monthly or annually. A small amount of the premium goes to secure life insurance and rest of the money is invested just like a mutual fund does. Policyholder goes on investing through the term of the policy – 5, 10 or 15 years and accumulates the units.

When you make an investment in ULIP, the insurance company invests part of the premium in shares/bonds etc., and the balance amount is utilized in providing an insurance cover. There are fund managers in the insurance companies who manage the investments and therefore the investor is spared the hassle of tracking the investments.

ULIPS allow you to switch your portfolio between debt and equity based on your risk appetite as well as your knowledge of the market's performance. Benefits like these which offer investors the flexibility of switching is a huge factor contributing to the popularity of these investment instruments.

Lock in period: One of the changes brought about by the Insurance Regulatory and Development Authority of India (IRDAI) in the year 2010 as regards ULIPs, was to increase the lock in a period from 3 years to 5 years. However, insurance being a long-term product, as an investor you may not really reap the benefits of the policy unless you hold it for the entire term of the policy which can range from 10 to 15 years.

Types of ULIPs: ULIPs are categorized based on the following broad parameters:

Funds that ULIPs invest in
a) Equity Funds: Where the premium paid is invested in the equity market and thereby is subject to higher risk.
b) Balanced funds: Where the premium paid is balanced between the debt and the equity market to minimize the risk for investors.
c) Debt Funds: Where the premium is invested in debt instruments which carry a lower risk but in turn also offer a lower return.

End use of Funds
Retirement Planning: For those of you who plan to invest for the retirement days while you are still employed.
Child Education: You can invest with a long-term goal of saving to fund your child's education or save for some unforeseen circumstances.

Death benefit to Policy Holders

a) Type I ULIP: This pays higher of the assured sum value or the fund value to the nominee in case of death of the policyholder.
b) Type II ULIP: This pays the assured sum value, plus the fund value to the nominee in case of the death of the policyholder.

Insurance Related Acts: Insurance Act, 1938: The Act applies to the General Insurance Corporation of India and the four Subsidiary companies subject to exceptions, restrictions and limitations as specified by the Central Government under powers conferred by Section 35 of the General Insurance Business (Nationalization) Act. The important provisions of the Act relate, among other things, to registrations, accounts and returns, investments, limitations in expenses of Management, prohibition of rebates, powers of investigation, licensing of agents, licensing of surveyors, advance payment of premium and Tariff Advisory Committee etc.

Marine Insurance Act, 1963: This Act codifies the law relating to Marine Insurance. With a few exceptions, this Act closely follows the UK Marine Insurance Act, 1906.

Motor Vehicles Act, 1939: According to this Act, no motor vehicle can be used in public places unless there is, in force, in relation to that vehicle, a policy of insurance issued by an authorized insurer.

Motor Vehicles Act, 1988: The Motor Vehicles (Amendment) Act, 1988 has introduced changes which have far- reaching consequences. The changes also affect Third Party Liability arising out of the use of the Motor Vehicles in a public place.

Workmen Compensation Act, 1923: The Act provides for the payment of compensation by employers to their workmen for injury by accident arising out of and in the course of employment.

The Carriage of Goods by Sea Act, 1925: The act specifies the minimum rights, liabilities and immunities of a ship owner in respect of loss or damage to cargo carried.

The Merchant Shipping Act, 1958: It provides protection to ship owners. The ship owners liability arises up to certain maximum sums for certain losses, provided the incident giving rise such claims has arisen without the actual fault or priority of the ship owner, whether the claims relates to loss of life, personal injury, or damage to property on land or water. It also confers an obligation on the ship owner to send his ship to sea in a sea worthy and safe condition.

The Inland Steam Vessels Act, 1977: The act is in relation to the insurance of mechanically propelled vessels against third party risks. It makes the same insurance compulsory for owners or operators of inland vessels to insure against legal liability for death or bodily injury of third parties or of passengers carried for hire or reward and for damage to property of third parties. It prescribes the limits of the liability.

Consumer Protection Act, 1986: The objective to pass this act is to provide for better protection of the interests of consumers and for the settlement of consumers disputes. It is applicable to the buyers of goods and services.

Public Liability insurance act 1991: It deals with the immediate relief of the persons affected by accidents arising of hazardous substances. It also does that this liability, which is on "no limit" basis has to be compulsorily insured.

Khan Working Group Committee	Development of Financial Institutions
Malegam Committee	Reforms in the primary market & Repositioning of UTI
Malhotra Committee	Broad Framework of insurance sector
Parekh Committee	Infrastructure Refinancing
Dilip C Chakraborty Committee	Help in implementing the new risk-based capital regime and it will also enhance protection policy holders
G.V Ramakrishnan Committee	On Disinvestment
Suresh Mathur	To review Micro Insurance Framework
Suresh Mathur	Reviewing norms related to insurance marketing firms

Amitabh Chaudhary	Analysis of the existing framework of IRDA linked and non-linked insurance product regulations
JJ Irani committee	Company Law Reforms

Insurance Company	Headquarters	Taglines/Slogans
Apollo Munich Health Insurance	Hyderabad	We Know Healthcare
Aviva India Life Insurance	Gurugram	Kal Par Control
Bajaj Alliance Life Insurance Company Limited	Pune	Jiyo Befiqar
Birla Sun Life Insurance Company Limited	Mumbai	Your Dreams Our Commitment
Cholamandalam MS General Insurance	Chennai	Trust, Transparency and Technology
Future Generali Life Insurance	Mumbai	Total Insurance Solutions / Ek Shaagun Zindagi Ke Naam
General Insurance Company	Mumbai	Aapatkale Rakshisyami
HDFC Standard Life Insurance Company Limited	Mumbai	Sar Utha Ke Jiyo
ICICI Lombard General Insurance Company Limited	Mumbai	Quick Easy Smart
ICICI Prudential Life Insurance Company Limited	Mumbai	Zimmedari ka Humsafar
IFFCO Tokio General Insurance	Gurugram	Muskurate Raho
Kotak Mahindra Old Mutual Life Insurance Limited	Mumbai	Faidey ka Insurance
Life Insurance Corporation (LIC) Limited	Mumbai	Yogaksheman Vahamyaham
Max Bupa Health Insurance	New Delhi	Your Health First
Max Life Insurance Company Limited	New Delhi	Aapke Sachhee Advisor
National Insurance Company Limited	Kolkata	Trusted Since 1906, Thoda Simple Socho
Oriental Insurance Company Limited	New Delhi	Prithivi, Agni, Jal, Akash, Sabhi Suraksha Hamare Pass.
PNB Metlife India Insurance Company Ltd.	Mumbai	Have You Met Life Today?
Sahara India Life Insurance Co. Limited	Lucknow	Chiranjivi Bhava
SBI Life Insurance Company Limited	Mumbai	With Us, You Are Sure
Shriram Life Insurance Company Ltd.	Hyderabad	Your Partner for Prosperity
Tata AIA Life Insurance Company Limited	Mumbai	You Click, We Cover
The New India Assurance Corporation Limited	Mumbai	India's Premier General Insurance Company
United India Insurance Company Limited	Chennai	Rest Assured With Us

FINANCIAL MANAGEMENT

Financial management is about controlling the flow of money in and out of the organization. Financial management is all about monitoring, controlling, protecting, and reporting on a company's financial resources.

Companies have accountants or finance teams responsible for managing their finances, including all bank transactions, loans, debts, investments, and other sources of funding. Finance teams are also responsible for ensuring the company follows all regulations, stays solvent, and is as profitable as possible.

Financial management is based on three broad financial decisions. What are these?

Ans: Financial management refers to the efficient acquisition, allocation and usage of funds of the company. It deals in three main dimensions of financial decisions namely, Investment decisions, Financial decisions and Dividend decisions.

Investment Decisions: Investment decisions refer to the decisions regarding where to invest so as to earn the highest possible returns on investment. Investment decisions can be taken for both long term as well as short term.

Long term investment decisions also known as Capital Budgeting decisions affect a business' long term earning capacity and profitability. For example, investment in a new machine, purchase of a new building, etc. are long term investment decisions.

Short term investment decisions also known as working capital decisions affect a business' day to day working operations. For example, decisions regarding cash or bill receivables are short term investment decisions.

Financial Decisions: Such decisions involve identifying various sources of funds and deciding the best combination for raising the funds. The main sources for raising funds are shareholders' funds (referred as equity) and borrowed funds (referred as debt). Based on the cost involved, risk and profitability a company must judiciously decide the combination of debt and equity to be used. For example, while debt is considered to be the cheapest source of finance, higher debt increases the financial risk. Financial decisions taken by a company affects its overall cost of capital and the financial risk.

Dividend Decisions: The decision involves the decision regarding the distribution of profit or surplus of the company. A company can distribute its profit to the equity share holders in the form of dividends or retain it with itself. Under dividend decision, a company decides what proportion of the surplus to distribute as dividends and what proportion to keep as retained earnings. It is aimed at maximising the shareholders' wealth while keeping in view the requirement of retained earnings that are needed for re-investment.

Two objectives of Financial Management:

Profit maximization: The main objective of financial management is profit maximization. The finance manager tries to earn maximum profits for the company in the short-term and the long-term. He cannot guarantee profits in the long term because of business uncertainties. However, a company can earn maximum profits even in the long-term, if:-

1.The Finance manager takes proper financial decisions.

2.He uses the finance of the company properly.

Wealth maximization: Wealth maximization (shareholders' value maximization) is also a main objective of financial management. Wealth maximization means to earn maximum wealth for the shareholders. So, the finance manager tries to give a maximum dividend to the shareholders. He also tries to increase the market value of the shares. The market value of the shares is directly related to the performance of the company. Better the performance, higher is the market value of shares and vice-versa. So, the finance manager must try to maximise shareholder's value.

Shareholders current wealth in the firm: Number of shares owned * current stock price per share.

Meaning Of Leverage: The word 'leverage', borrowed from physics, is frequently used in financial management.

The object of application of which is made to gain higher financial benefits compared to the fixed charges payable, as it happens in physics i.e., gaining larger benefits by using a lesser amount of force.

Leverage results from using borrowed capital as a funding source when investing to expand the firm's asset base and generate returns on risk capital.

Leverage is an investment strategy of using borrowed money - specifically, the use of various financial instruments or borrowed capital - to increase the potential return of an investment.

Leverage can also refer to the amount of debt a firm uses to finance assets. When one refers to a company, property or investment as "highly leveraged," it means that item has more debt than equity.

Definitions of Leverage: Some definitions are given to have a clear idea about leverage:

According to Ezra Solomon: "Leverage is the ratio of net returns on shareholders equity and the net rate of return on capitalisation".

According to J. C. Van Home: "Leverage is the employment of an asset or funds for which the firm pays a fixed cost of fixed return."

Types of Leverage: Leverage are the three types: (i) Operating leverage (ii) Financial leverage (iii) Combined leverage

Operating Leverage: Operating leverage refers to the use of fixed operating costs such as depreciation, insurance of assets, repairs and maintenance, property taxes etc. in the operations of a firm. But it does not include interest on debt capital. Higher the proportion of fixed operating cost as compared to variable cost, higher is the operating leverage, and vice versa. Degree of Operating Leverage: The earnings before interest and taxes (i.e., EBIT) changes with increase or decrease in the sales volume. Operating leverage is used to measure the effect of variation in sales volume on the level of EBIT. The formula used to compute operating leverage is:
Contribution = Contribution / Operating Profit
Where, Contribution = Sales - Variable Cost
Operating Profit = Sales - Variable Cost – Fixed Cost
Degree of Operating Leverage = Percentage change in profits / Percentage change in sales

Importance of Operating Leverage: 1. It gives an idea about the impact of changes in sales on theoperating income of the firm. 2. High degree of operating leverage magnifies the effect on EBIT for a small change in the sales volume. 3. Highdegreeof operating leverage indicates increase in operating profit or EBIT. 4. High operating leverage results from the existence of a higher amount of fixed costs in the total cost structure of a firm which makes the margin of safety low. 5. High operating leverage indicates higher amount of sales required to reach break-even point. 6. Higher fixed operating cost in the total cost structure of a firm promotes higher operating leverage and its operating risk. 7. A lower operating leverage gives enough cushion to the firm by providing a high margin of safety against variation in sales.

Financial Leverage: Financial leverage is primarily concerned with the financial activities which involve raising of funds from the sources for which a firm has to bear fixed charges such as interest expenses, loan fees etc. These sources include long-term debt (i.e., debentures, bonds etc.) and preference share capital. Degree of Financing Leverage: Financing leverage is a measure of changes in operating profit or EBIT on the levels of earning per share. It is computed as: Financial leverage = Percentage change in EPS / Percentage change in EBIT = Increase in EPS / EPS / Increase in EBIT/EBIT The financial leverage at any level of EBIT is called its degree. It is computed as ratio of EBIT to the profit before tax (EBT). Degree of Financial leverage (DFL) = EBIT / EBT The value of degree of financial leverage must be greater than 1. If the value of degree of financial leverage is 1, then there will be no financial leverage.

Degree of financial leverage = EBIT / EBIT- I
Or EBIT / EBT
Or OP / PBT
EBIT = Earning Before Interest and Tax or Operating Profit
EBT = Earning Before Tax or Profit Before Tax (PBT)
OP =Operating Profit (i.e. Contribution - Fixed cost)
I= Interest

The importance of financial leverage: 1. It helps the financial manager to design an optimum capital structure. The optimum capital structure implies that combination of debt and equity at which overall cost of capital is minimum and valueof the firm is maximum. 2. It increases earning per share (EPS) as well as financial risk. 3. A high financial leverage indicates existence of high financial fixed costs and high financial risk. 4. It helps to bring balance between financial risk and return in thecapital structure. 5. It shows theexcess on return on investment over the fixed coston theuseof the funds. 6. It is an important tool in the hands of the finance manager while determining the amount of debt in the capital structure of the firm.

Difference between Operating Leverage and Financial Leverage:
Operating leverage is related to the firm's operating cost structure while financial leverage is related to the firm's capital structure.

Operating Leverage is helpful in measuring the business risk of the firm while Financial Leverage is helpful in measuring the financial risk of the firm.

Operating Leverage is determined by the relationship between Sales revenue and EBIT (Operating Income) of the firm while Financial Leverage is determined by the relationship between EBIT (Operating Income) and EPS (Earning Per Share) of the firm.

Higher Degree of Operating Leverage (DOL) shows the higher degree of Business risk to the firm while Higher Degree of Financial Leverage (DFL) shows the higher degree of financial risk of the firm.

Combined Leverage: Operating leverage shows the operating risk and is measured by the percentage change in EBIT due to percentage change in sales. The financial leverage shows the financial risk and is measured by the percentage change in EPS dueto percentage change in EBIT. The Combined Leverage can be measured with the help Of the following formula: Combined Leverage = Operating leverage * Financial leverage.

Importance Of Combined Leverage:
1.It indicates the effect that changes in sales will have on EPS.
2. It shows the combined effect of operating leverage and financial leverage.
3. A combination of high operating leverage and a high financial leverage is a very risky situation because the combined effect of the two leverages is a multiple of these two leverages.
4. A combination of high operating leverage and a low financial leverage indicates that the management should be careful as the high risk involved in the former is balanced by the later.
5. A combination of low operating leverage and a high financial leverage gives a better situation for maximizing return and minimizing risk factor, because keeping the operating leverage at low rate full advantage of debt financing can be taken to maximize return. In this situation the firm reaches its BEP at a low level of saleswith minimum business risk.
6. A combination of low operating leverage and low financial leverage indicates that the firm loses profitable opportunities.

Conclusion:
In Leverage analysis, the main focus is on the measurement of the relationship between the two variables rather than measuring the variables. The Measurement of leverages is the technique used by the business firms to measure the Risk– Return

relationship of the firm's operating and financial activities.

Leverage is the term which is commonly used to describe the organization's ability to utilize the assets which are having fixed costs (or) different sources of funds to increase the returns to the firm.

It is important to timelyand accurate leverage analysis for the success of a firm.

The value of degree of financial leverage must be greater than 1. If the value of degree of financial leverage is 1, then there will be no financial leverage.

Capital Structure

The Capital Structure is the starting sum of money required to start basic company operations. To secure lasting financial support for a business, it requires gathering funds from various channels, forming what is termed as the capital structure. This serves as the fundamental framework in business finance, illustrating how diverse funding sources can be utilized to fuel expansion and sustain day-to-day operations.

Essentially, it signifies the mix or ratios of preference share capital, equity share capital, long-term loans, debentures, retained earnings, and other financial resources within the overall capital raised by a firm to manage its operations effectively.

Capital Structure Meaning: Capital structure refers to the blend of debt and/or equity utilized by a company to support its activities and fund its assets. This composition is commonly represented through ratios such as debt-to-equity or debt-to-capital. Businesses rely on both debt and equity capital to finance their operations, capital expenses, acquisitions, and various investments.

Capital Structure Formula: The method for calculating a company's capital structure, presented as a percentage, can be summarized as follows:
Capital Structure (%) = Percentage of Common Equity + Percentage of Debt + Percentage of Preferred Stock

Importance of Capital Structure: It plays a crucial role in a company's stability, and its significance is underscored by several key factors:

Enhanced Market Value: A solid capital setup boosts a company's market value, leading to higher prices for its shares and securities. This increased valuation is advantageous in the market.

Effective Fund Utilization: A well-structured capital setup ensures efficient use of available funds, preventing situations of over or under capitalization. This balance is vital for financial health.

Profit Maximization: A proper capital setup contributes to increased profits, providing higher returns to stakeholders. This financial efficiency is beneficial for both the company and its investors.

Optimized Capital Costs: By carefully managing the balance between debt and equity, a company can maximize shareholder capital while minimizing overall capital expenses. This strategic approach is essential for financial sustainability.

Flexibility: A sound capital setup offers companies the flexibility to adjust their debt levels according to specific situations, allowing for adaptable financial management.

Optimal Capital Structure: The optimal capital structure for a company is typically seen as the balance between debt and equity that leads to the lowest overall cost of capital, known as the weighted average cost of capital (WACC). Although this precise definition isn't always applied in real-world scenarios, companies often have their unique strategic or philosophical perspectives on what the perfect structure should be.

To achieve this optimum balance, a company can either issue more debt or equity. The additional capital obtained can be used to invest in new assets or to buy back existing debt or equity, a strategy known as **recapitalization**.

Types of Capital Structure: Capital structure is essentially the arrangement of long-term funding from various sources, primarily categorized into two major types: equity and debt. Businesses gather funds through different means, including preference shares, equity shares, retained earnings, and long-term loans, all with the aim of sustaining their operations.

Equity Capital: Equity capital encompasses the financial resources owned by the shareholders or proprietors and comes in two distinct forms:

A) Retained Earnings: These are profits set aside by the organization to fortify its financial standing.

B) Contributed Capital: This refers to the funds invested by the company's owners during its inception or received from shareholders in exchange for ownership stakes in the company.

Debt Capital: Debt capital, on the other hand, refers to borrowed funds employed within the business, and it can take various forms:

A) Long-Term Bonds: These bonds are considered the most secure form of debt due to their extended repayment timeline, with only interest payments required until the principal is repaid at maturity.

B) Short-Term Commercial Paper: This represents a short-term debt instrument used by companies to raise capital for brief durations.

Factors Influencing Capital Structure: Several factors play a pivotal role in determining a company's capital structure:

Costs of Capital: This refers to the expenses incurred in acquiring funds from various sources. A business must generate enough revenue to cover these costs and facilitate its growth.

Degree of Control: The type of shareholders and the extent of their voting rights significantly influence a firm's capital structure. Equity shareholders hold more power in a company compared to preference or debenture shareholders, shaping the overall structure.

Trading on Equity: When a company relies heavily on equity financing to borrow new funds and increase returns, it engages in trading on equity. This occurs when the return on total capital surpasses the interest rates on debentures or newly borrowed debt.

Government Policies: Capital structure decisions are also impacted by government regulations and policies. Changes in monetary and fiscal policies can lead to alterations in a company's capital structure choices.

What is over-capitalisation?

Ans.Over-capitalisation' refers to that state of affairs where actual profits of a company are not sufficient to pay interest and dividend at proper rates. In other words, a company is over-capitalised when it is unable to pay a fair return on its investment.

Real value < Book value = Over-capitalisation

Real value is market Value.

Elaborate on the meaning of under-capitalisation.

Ans. Under-capitalisation refers to the effective and optimum utilization of funds employed in a business. Thus, when a company succeeds in earning abnormally large income continuously for a pretty long time, symptoms of under-capitalisation gradually develop in the company. The market value of shares of an under-capitalised company exceeds its book value.

To sum up, we can say that,

Real value > Book value = Under-capitalisation.

What is the cost of capital?

Ans. The cost of capital is the rate of return which the company has to pay to various suppliers of funds in the company. There is variation in the cost of capital due to the fact that different kinds of investment carry different levels of risk, which is compensated for by different levels of return on the investment.

What are the elements of cost of capital?

Ans. The cost of capital consists of the following elements :

a) Cost of Equity (Ke)

b) Cost of Retained Earnings (Kq)

c) Cost of Preferred Capital (Kp)

d) Cost of Debt (Kd)

What are the different types of cost? Or explain various concepts of cost of capital.

Ans. Cost can be classified into the following types:

a) Historical cost and future cost: The costs which are related to the past are called historical costs. They are referred to as book costs and are estimated costs for the future. These costs are considered to be quite relevant in financial decisions.

b) Specific cost and composite cost: The cost of a specific source of capital is referred to as specific cost whereas the combination of the cost of various sources of capital is called combined cost. It refers to the weighted average cost of capital.

c) Explicit cost and implicit cost: An explicit cost refers to the discount rate equalizing the present value of cash inflows with the present value of cash outflows. In other words, it refers to the internal rate of return. Implicit cost refers to the cost of the opportunity foregone to take up a particular project. It is also known as opportunity cost.

d) Average cost and marginal cost: The combined cost of various sources of capital like debentures, preference shares and equity shares is referred to as average cost. Whereas, the average cost of capital incurred to acquire additional funds needed by a firm is called marginal cost.

Some of the major different theories of dividend in financial management are as follows: 1. Walter's model 2. Gordon's model 3. Modigliani and Miller's hypothesis.

1. Walter's model: Professor James E. Walterargues that the choice of dividend policies almost always affects the value of the enterprise. His model shows clearly the importance of the relationship between the firm's internal rate of return (r) and its cost of capital (k) in determining the dividend policy that will maximize the wealth of shareholders. Walter's model is based on the following assumptions:

1. The firm finances all investment through retained earnings; that is debt or new equity is not issued.

2. The firm's internal rate of return (r), and its cost of capital (k) are constant.

3. All earnings are either distributed as dividend or reinvested internally immediately.

4. Beginning earnings and dividends never change. The values of the earnings per share (E), and the dividend per share (D) may be changed in the model to determine results, but any given values of E and D are assumed to remain constant forever in determining a given value.

5. The firm has a very long or infinite life.

Walter's formula to determine the market price per share (P) is as follows:

$$P = D/K + r(E-D)/K/K$$

2. Gordon's Model: One very popular model explicitly relating the market value of the firm to dividend policy is developed by Myron Gordon.

Assumptions: Gordon's model is based on the following assumptions.

1. The firm is an all Equity firm

2. No external financing is available

3. The internal rate of return (r) of the firm is constant.

4. The appropriate discount rate (K) of the firm remains constant.

5. The firm and its stream of earnings are perpetual

6. The corporate taxes do not exist.

7. The retention ratio (b), once decided upon, is constant. Thus, the growth rate (g) = br is constant forever.

8. K > br = g if this condition is not fulfilled, we cannot get a meaningful value for the share.

According to Gordon's dividend capitalisation model, the market value of a share (Pq) is equal to the present value of an infinite stream of dividends to be received by the share. Thus:

$$Po: E1(1-b)/K-br$$

3. Modigliani and Miller's hypothesis: According to Modigliani and Miller (M-M), dividend policy of a firm is irrelevant as it does not affect the wealth of the shareholders. They argue that the value of the firm depends on the firm's earnings which result from its investment policy. Thus, when the investment decision of the firm is given, the dividend decision, the split of earnings between dividends and retained earnings, is of no significance in determining the value of the firm. M – M's hypothesis of irrelevance is based on the following assumptions.

1. The firm operates in perfect capital market
2. Taxes do not exist
3. The firm has a fixed investment policy
4. Risk of uncertainty does not exist. That is, investors are able to forecast future prices and dividends with certainty and one discount rate is appropriate for all securities and all time periods.

Thus, $r = K = Kt$ for all t.

Po: $D1 + P1/ 1 + K$

What do you mean by the term 'dividend'?

Ans. The term 'dividend' refers to that portion of profit (after tax) which is distributed among the owners/ shareholders of the firm.

According to S.M. Shah, "Dividends are profits of a trading company divided amongst members in proportion to their shares. " According to the Supreme Court of India, "Dividend is that portion of profits of the çompany which is allocated to the holders of shares in the company.

What are the different forms in which dividend can be distributed?

Ans. Dividends can be distributed in a number of forms, such as:

1) Cash dividend: It is the usual and most popular method of paying dividends. Cash dividend gives an opportunity to the
shareholders to invest the cash in any manner they desire and these are mainly distributed by the companies having sound liquidity position.

2) Stock dividend: Bonus shares are referred to as stock dividends. The capitalisation of reserves and surpluses by a company when it has surplus resources but inadequate liquidity is known as bonus shares.

3) Bond dividend: The company distributes dividends in the form of bonds or debentures payable after 5 to 7 years. The bond dividend is distributed when the company falls short of liquidity and it is not in a position to distribute dividend in cash.

4) Property dividend : Property dividend is not a popular practice in India. Property dividends are distributed in the form of certain assets except cash under exceptional circumstances.

5) Scrip dividend: Scrip dividend is paid when the liquidity position of the company is weak. Shareholders are issued shares or debentures of other companies held by the company as investment. This type of dividend payment is not allowed after passing of the Companies (Amendment) Act, 1960.

What is dividend policy?

Ans. Dividend policy deals with determining the amount of dividend and planning its distribution pattern. A company should formulate a sound dividend policy by taking into consideration the following factors:

Past dividend.

Present year profits.

Liquidity position.

Financial health of the company, etc.

What are the different types of dividend policy?

Ans: The different types of dividend policies are :

1) Constant payout ratio policy: In this policy, the company pays a fixed percentage of the net earnings every year. Thus under this policy, dividend per share and retained earnings change, from year to year with the changes in earnings of the company, but the dividend payout ratio remains stable. Very few firms select this method.

2) Constant Dividend Ratio Policy: Under this policy, dividend is paid at a constant rate even when earnings vary from year to year. This policy is possible only through the maintenance of "Dividend Equalisation Reserve". The company then invests funds equal to such reserves in some current investments so as to manage the liquidity of the necessary funds in times of need. Firms are, generally, careful to set the dividend at a sustáinable level and raise it only when the firm can sustain the higher level.

3) Multiple dividend increase policy: Under this policy. there is very frequent and small amount of increase in dividend to give the illusion of movement and growth. The objective behind such a policy is that the market rewards consistently increase.

4) Regular dividend plus extra dividend policy: Under this policy, an extra dividend is paid to the shareholders in addition to the regular dividend paid by the company. This dividend is generally paid during the period of prosperity, i.e. for a short period only.

5) Uniform cash dividend plus bonus share policy: Under this policy, a minimum rate of dividend per share is paid in cash plus bonus shares are issued out of accumulated reserves. The issue of bonus shares is not annually. It depends on the amount kept in reserves over a period say 3 to 5 years.

Working Capital: Meaning, Importance and Types. Working capital is an indicator of the short-term financial position that measures the overall efficiency of an organization. It is calculated by subtracting current liabilities from current assets and listed directly in its balance sheet.

Current assets mean the money kept in a bank and assets that can be converted into cash in case if any situation arises. Current liabilities represent debt that an individual will pay within the prescribed year. Finally, working capital is the money left after subtracting liabilities from an individual's money in the bank.

Current assets consist of cash, accounts receivable, and inventory. Current liabilities include wages, taxes, interest owed.

In broader terms, working capital is also used to measure the company's financial health. If there is a larger difference between what a company owns and what an individual owns for the short-term, the business will be healthier.

If the company owes more than they own, they will have negative working capital, and their business might get closed.

Why Is Working Capital Essential?
The sole purpose of using working capital is to fund operations, meet the short-term obligation, and continue to have sufficient working capital. It's continuously paying its employees and suppliers to meet other obligations like taxes and interest payments even if they have any cash flow challenges. Working capital is also used to fuel business growth without incurring debt. If the company does not want to take a loan, they can qualify easily for loans or other forms of credit because of their positive working capital.

Several financial teams have mainly two goals in their mind:

1) To have a clear goal and view of how much cash is on hand at any given time

2) To work with multiple businesses and to maintain enough working capital to cover liabilities.

Types Of Working Capital
The types of working capital are mainly divided into different parts:

Gross Working Capital: Gross working capital is the total value of the company's current assets. Current assets include cash, receivables, short-term investments, and especially market securities.

The Gross working capital does not showcase the current liabilities. Gross working capital can be executed by calculating the difference between the existing assets and current liabilities.

The difference remaining is the actual working capital that the company has to meet its obligations.

Net Working Capital: Networking capital is the difference between the current assets and current liabilities of the company. If the company's assets are more than current liabilities, it indicates a positive working capital, and the company is in a financial position to meet its obligations.

However, if the company's assets are less than current liabilities, it indicates a negative working capital, and the company is facing financial distress.

The key difference between gross and net working capital is that gross working capital will always be a positive value. In contrast, networking capital can either be a negative or positive value.

Permanent Working Capital: Permanent working capital is the minimum amount of capital required to carry on the operations without interruption or difficulty.

For example, a company will need minimum cash to keep the operations smooth and running; here, the minimum amount of money required will act as permanent working capital.

Regular Working Capital: Regular working capital is the amount of funds businesses require to fund its day to day operations. For example, cash needed for making payment of wages, raw materials, salaries comes under regular working capital.

Reserve Margin Working Capital: Apart from conducting day-to-day activities, a business may need some amount of capital to face unforeseen circumstances. Reserve margin working capital is nothing, but the money kept aside apart from the regular working capital. These funds are held separately against unexpected events like floods, natural calamities, storms, etc.

Variable Working Capital: Variable working capital can be defined as the capital invested for a temporary period in the business. Variable working capital is also called fluctuating working capital.

Such capital differs with respect to changes in the business assets or the size of the business. Furthermore, variable capital is subdivided into two parts:

1) Seasonable Variable Working Capital: Seasonable variable working capital is the amount of capital kept aside to meet the seasonal demand if the business is running seasonally.

2) Special Variable Working Capital: Special variable working capital is the temporary rise in the working capital due to any unforeseen or occurrence of a special event.

Capital budgeting is made up of two words 'capital' and 'budgeting.' In this context, capital expenditure is the spending of funds for large expenditures like purchasing fixed assets and equipment, repairs to fixed assets or equipment, research and development,

expansion and the like. Budgeting is setting targets for projects to ensure maximum profitability.

Capital budgeting is a process of evaluating investments and huge expenses in order to obtain the best returns on investment.

Capital Budgeting Techniques: To assist the organization in selecting the best investment there are various techniques available based on the comparison of cash inflows and outflows. **These techniques are:**

Payback period method: In this technique, the entity calculates the time period required to earn the initial investment of the project or investment. The project or investment with the shortest duration is opted for.

Net Present value: The net present value is calculated by taking the difference between the present value of cash inflows and the present value of cash outflows over a period of time. The investment with a positive NPV will be considered. In case there are multiple projects, the project with a higher NPV is more likely to be selected.

Accounting Rate of Return: In this technique, the total net income of the investment is divided by the initial or average investment to derive at the most profitable investment.

Internal Rate of Return (IRR): For NPV computation a discount rate is used. IRR is the rate at which the NPV becomes zero. The project with higher IRR is usually selected.

Profitability Index: Profitability Index is the ratio of the present value of future cash flows of the project to the initial investment required for the project. Each technique comes with inherent advantages and disadvantages. An organization needs to use the best-suited technique to assist it in budgeting. It can also select different techniques and compare the results to derive the best profitable projects.

FILL IN THE BLANKS:

1. Financial management suffers from lack of __
Ans. objectivity
2. Profit maximization is a _____ concept.
Ans. vague
3. Wealth maximization incorporates _____ value of money.
Ans. time
4. The traditional approach to finance function ignores _____.
Ans. internal decision-making
5. If there is no fixed cost, there will be no
Ans. financial leverage
6. Degree of financial leverage = _____ / PBT.
Ans: OP
7. Capitalization is a _____ scope than capital structure.
Ans. wider
8. Retained earnings comprise _____.
Ans. opportunity cost
9. Capital budgeting involves _____ decisions.
Ans. irreversible
10. Pay-back reciprocal = Annual cash flow / ?
Ans. Total investment
11. In the NPV method, ranking of projects depends on _____.
Ans. discount rate
12. Special working capital is a part of _____ working capital.
Ans. variable
13. The rate of dividend payout ratio should be initial stage of company.
Ans. moderate
14. Constant dividend rate policy is possible only through the maintenance of
Ans. dividend equalization reserve
15. A new company will follow a _____ dividend policy.
Ans. rigid

STATE WHETHER THE FOLLOWING STATEMENTS ARE TRUE OR FALSE:

1. Financial management is an indispensable organ.
Ans. True
2. In the traditional approach, finance means cash only.
Ans. False
3. Profit maximization is not justified on the ground of rationality.
Ans. False
4. Profit maximization ignores the short-run concept.
Ans. False
5. Financial leverage is present if there is fixed cost capital.
Ans. True
6. With increase in financial leverage, value of firm increases.
Ans. True
7. Share premium is a debt capital.
Ans. False
8. Explicit cost refers to the internal rate of return.
Ans. True
9. Funds in capital budgeting are invested in flexible activities.
Ans. True
10. When the cost of projects differs insignificantly, the profitability index method is not suitable.
Ans: True
11. Depreciation funds are an internal source of working capital.
Ans. True
12. Lower the scale of operation, higher is the need of working capital.
Ans. False
13. Scrip dividend is paid when the liquidity position of the company is weak.
Ans. True
14. Under uniform cash dividend plus bonus share policy, bonus shares are given annually.
Ans. False
15. During periods of boom, high rates of dividends are paid to market the securities.
Ans. True

Multiple Choice Questions

1.Which of the following is not a finance function?
(a) Recurring finance function
(b) Routine function
(c) Advisory function
(d) Accounting function *

2.The most complex task of a finance manager is to
(a) increase profitability of the business
(b) raise funds for the business
(c) strike a balance between profitability and liquidity of the business. *

(d) ensure effective utilization of the procured fund.
3.Finance means
(a) money
(b) cash *
(c) credit
(d) fund

4.One of the limitations of profit maximization is that it is
(a) a preceptive idea
(b) a vague concept *
(c) not a socially desirable objective
(d) a long run concept.

5.Leverage is of _____ types.
(a) 2
(b) 3 *
(c) 4
(d) 6

6.Contribution =
(a) Sales + Variable Cost + Fixed costH
(b) Sales- Variable Cost - Fixed Cost
(c) Sales - Variable Cost *
(d) Sales + Variable Cost

7. Financial leverage =
(a) EBIT / EBIT -I * 100 *
(b) EBT / EBIT * 100

8. Composite leverage =

(a) Operating leverage x Financial leverage *
(b) Operating leverage - Financial leverage
(c) Operating leverage + Financial leverage
(d) all of the above

9. The different forms of capital structure are
(a) equity shares
(b) equity and preference shares
(c) equity shares and debentures
(d) all of the above *

10. Balanced capital structure' is also known as
(a) equivalent capital structure
(b) optimal capital structure *
(c) indifference capital structure
(d) none of the above

11. Cost of capital' comprises _____
(a) cost of equity (k)
(b) cost of preferred capital (k,)
(c) cost of debt (k,)
(d) all of the above *

12. Retained earnings comprises _____ cost
(a) historical
(b) opportunity *
(c) specific
(d) explicit

13. Which of the following is not a principle of capital budgeting
(a) Huge amount of funds
(b) Investment of fund
(c) Procurement of funds *
(d) Exchange of current funds

14. Which of the following is not a type of capital budgeting proposals?
(a) Dependent proposals
(b) Independent proposals
(c) Mutually inclusive proposals *
(d) Mutually exclusive proposal

15. The excess of current assets over current liabilities is known as
(a) reserved capital
(b) working capital
(c) nominal capital *
(d) none of the above

16. Mathematically, operating cycle period =
(a) R t W +F + D-C *
(b) R- W+F+D-C
(c) R + W+F+ D+C
(d) E+ W+F-D –C

17. Which of the following is not a form of dividend?
(a) Cash dividend
(b) Stock dividend *
(c) Credit dividend
(d) Bond dividend

18. Bonus shares is a form of _____ dividend.
(a) stock *
(b) scrip
(c) bond
(d) property

19. Over-capitalization =
(a) Real value <Book value *
(b) Real value >Book value
(c) Real value = Book value
(d) None of the above.

20. The equation 'Real Value > Book value' indicates
(a) over capitalization
(b) under-capitalization *
(c) fair cap
(d) none

21. Dividend is paid to
(a) directors
(b) shareholders *
(c) employees
(d) managers

Here we have listed the Acts related to banking sector.

1. Negotiable Instrument Act-1881
2. The Bankers' Books Evidence Act-1891
3. The Reserve Bank of India Act-1934
4. The Industrial Finance Corporation of India Act-1948
5. The Banking Companies (Legal Practitioner Clients' Accounts) Act-1949
6. The Industrial Disputes (Banking and Insurance Companies) Act-1949
7. The Banking Regulation (Companies) Rules-1949
8. The Banking Regulation Act-1949
9. The State Financial Corporations Act-1951
10. The Reserve Bank of India (Amendment and Misc. Provisions) Act-1953
11. The Industrial Disputes (Banking Companies) Decision Act-1955
12. The State Bank of India Act-1955
13. The State Bank of India (Subsidiary Banks) Act-1959
14. The Subsidiary Banks General Regulation-1959
15. The Deposit Insurance and Credit Guarantee Corporation Act-1961 (DICGC)
16. The Banking Companies (Acquisition and Transfer of Undertakings) Act-1970
17. The Regional Rural Banks Act-1976
18. The Banking Companies (Acquisition and Transfer of Undertakings) Act-1980
19. The Export-Import Bank of India Act-1981
20. The National Bank for Agriculture and Rural Development Act-1981
21. Chit Fund Act-1982
22. Sick Industrial Companies (Special Provisions) Act-1985
23. The National Housing Bank Act-1987
24. SIDBI Act-1989
25. The Special Court (trial of Offences relating to Transactions in Securities) Act-1992
26. The Industrial Finance Corporation (Transfer of Undertakings and Repeal) Act-1993
27. Industrial Reconstruction Bank (Transfer of Undertaking & Appeal) Act-1997

28. The Securitization and Reconstruction of Financial Assets and Enforcement of Security Interest Act-(SARFASI-2002)

29. Industrial Development Bank (Transfer of Undertaking & Repeal) Act-2003

30. Credit Information Companies (Rules & Regulation) Act-2005

31. The Industrial Finance Corporation of India Act-1948

32. The Banking Companies (Legal Practitioner Clients' Accounts) Act-1949

33. The Industrial Disputes (Banking and Insurance Companies) Act-1949

34. The State Financial Corporations Act-1951

35. The Reserve Bank of India (Amendment and Misc. Provisions) Act-1953

36. The Industrial Disputes (Banking Companies) Decision Act-1955

37. The State Bank of India Act-1955

38. The State Bank of India (Subsidiary Banks) Act-1959

39. The Subsidiary Banks General Regulation-1959

40. The Deposit Insurance and Credit Guarantee Corporation Act 1961

41. The National Bank for Agriculture and Rural Development Act-1981

42. Chit Fund Act-1982

43. Shipping Development Fund Committee (Abolition)Act-1985

44. Sick Industrial Companies (Special Provisions) Act-1985

45. The National Housing Bank Act-1987

46. The Special Court (trial of Offences relating to Transactions in Securities) Act-1992

47. The Industrial Finance Corporation (Transfer of Undertakings and Repeal) Act-1993

48. Industrial Reconstruction Bank (Transfer of Undertaking & Appeal) Act-1997

49. SIDBI General Regulations, 1990

50. Banking Regulation (Companies) Rules 1949

51. The Nationalized Banks (Management and Misc. Provisions) Scheme, 1970

52. NABARD General Regulations 1982

53. Banking Companies (Period of Preservation of Records) Rules, 1985

54. Banking Companies (Regulation) Rules, 1985

55. NABARD Bonds Regulations - 1988

56. The Banking Ombudsman Scheme, 2006

57. Factoring Act Rules, 2011

58. SARFAESI (Central registry) Rules, 2011

59. Banker's Books Evidence Act, 1891

60. Banking Regulation Act, 1949

61. Banking Companies (Legal Practitioners' Clients' Account) Act, 1949

62. Banking Regulation (Companies) Rules, 1949

63. Banking Companies (Acquisition and Transfer of Undertaking) Act, 1969

64. Debts Recovery Appellate Tribunal (Procedure) Rules, 1994

65. Foreign Contribution (Regulation) Act, 1976

66. Foreign Exchange Management Act, 1999

67. Indian Partnership Act, 1932

68. Indian Stamp Act, 1899

69. Indian Trusts Act, 1882

70. Limitation Act, 1963

71. Recovery of Debts due to Banks and Financial Institutions Act, 1993

72. Reserve Bank of India Act - 1934

FINANCIAL SERVICES

What do you mean by financial services?
Ans: The term 'financial services' refer to a variety of businesses or services that deal in merchant banking, credit card companies,
consumer finance companies, stock brokerage or with money management. These include all services and products offered by money market as well as capital market organisations to the public. For example: banks, credit card companies, insurance companies, asset management firms, investment companies, etc.

What do you mean by Finance?
Ans: Finance means funding. Finance means funds that are required to support an enterprise. The requirement of funds, management of funds to support, to investment, in terms to providing credit etc.

What are the providers and users of financial services?
Ans: The providers of financial services are:
(1) Capital market intermediaries: They provide long-term funds and are composed of term lending institutions and investing institutions.
(2) Money market intermediaries: They provide short-term funds and are composed of commercial banks, co-operative banks, etc.
The users of financial services are:
a) Individuals and
b) Corporate customers.

Types of financial services:

1) Lease financing: Lease is an important form of financing employed to meet the intermediate and long-term needs of corporate enterprises along with deriving the use of an asset for a stated period of time without getting its ownership. It facilitates a firm to use a fixed asset on payment of contractual, periodic and tax-deductible payment. The lessor is the owner of the asset, and the lessee is the receiver of the services or the asset or the user of the asset under the lease contract, Thus, a relationship of tenancy exists between the tenant and the Landlord. The consideration paid by the lessee is called rent.

2) Hire purchase and consumer credit: Hire purchase is a system in which the buyer acquires immediate possession of goods on payment of a periodical installment, but the ownership of such goods passes to the buyer only after the payment of last installment.

Consumer credit, on the other hand is a type of financial service in which the consumer pays only a part of the cash purchase price at the time of delivery of the asset (generally durable consumer goods) and the balance amount along with interest over a certain specified period of time. Consumer credit are mostly provided by Commercial banks, financial companies, foreign or multinational banks, etc. However, consumer credit is not under the purview of any legislative regulation in India.

3) Factoring and forfeiting: Factoring is a collection and financial service, involving a continuous arrangement between a financial intermediary known as the factor and a business concern, i.e. the client. In factoring, the factor purchases the client's account receivables / book debts either with or without recourse to the client, with an objective to improve the client's (seller's) cash flow, by converting his credit sales invoices into ready cash. In other words, factoring is an activity of managing trade debts of a business concern through controlling credit extended to the customers and administering sales ledger by the factor.

Factoring refers to the financial option for the management of receivables. It is the concession of credit sales into cash. Factoring functions in a manner where a financial institution (factor) buys accounts receivable of a company (client) and pays up to 80% or 90% of the amount immediately on agreement. Factoring company pays remaining balance to the client when the Customer pays the debt. Various examples of factoring are factoring for goods/products purchased, factoring, for construction services, factoring against medical insurance, etc.

The mechanism of factoring involves the following steps:

Step (i): An order for goods or services on credit is placed by the customer with the client. The goods are delivered to the customer along with an invoice.

Step (ii): The factor is assigned with invoice by the client.

Step (iii) : The factor makes pre-payment to the client upto 80% of the invoice and sends periodical statements.

Step (iv): The factor sends monthly statement of accounts to customer and follow-up.

Step(v): The customer then makes payment to the factor.

Step (vi): On realization of the amount, the factor makes balance 20 percent to the client.

Forfeiting refers to 100 percent discounting (purchase) of international trade receivables without recourse to the exporter. It transforms the exporter's credit transaction into a cash sale. As a result, the exporters are protected from all the risks associated with selling overseas on credit.

4) Bill discounting: Bill discounting is a type of lending in which the bank takes the bill drawn by the drawer on his drawee (customer) and pays him immediately after deducting commission on the due date. The banker collects the total amount by presenting the bill to the drawee. However, the amount of advance offered by bank greatly depends on the past record and reputation of the drawee.

The essential conditions to be fulfilled for bills discounting are:

a) The bill must be a documentary bill.

b) It must have been duly accepted.

c) It must bear at least two authorised signatures.

d) Generally, trade bills are discounted by banks.

5) Venture capital financing: Venture capital is a form of equity financing designed especially for funding high risk and high reward projects. It is useful for financing high technology projects and helps to convert research and development into production. It is an instrument in new

enterprises lacking a stable record of growth. Venture capital can be provided to any single entrepreneur or a small-scale enterprise having a unique idea or a technology. It only concerns the idea or technology, which it has financed and should sell in future, ie. it should imply

growth for venture capital equity invested in the said enterprise. As the idea and technology will become successful and commercial in future, the small entrepreneur and his enterprise will also grow into large ones.

6) Custodial services: Custodial services is about providing safe-keeping and clearing services to institutional investors like FII's (foreign institutional investors) and mutual funds. This business requires presence of global networking for catering to foreign investors In India, any bank which wants to provide custodial services have to be registered with SEBI (under SEBI, Custodian of Securities Regulations, 1996) before commencement of business Services provided by a bank custodian are typically the settlement, safekeeping and

reporting of customer's marketable securities and cash.

7) Credit rating: Credit rating is a formal assessment of the ability of a borrower to repay the loan. It analyses borrower's credit quality to discharge the debts as per terms of issue. It serves as an indicator of the relative capacity of the borrowing entity to repay its debt obligation within a specified time period. It is neither a general purpose evaluation nor overall assessment of credit risk of a firm. An agency which performs this functions is called credit rating agency.

8) Merchant banking: Merchant banking is an institution which covers a wide range of activities like management of customer services, portfolio management, credit syndication, acceptance of credit, counselling, insurance, etc. Merchant banking is a

combination of banking and consultancy services. It provides consultancy, to its clients, for financial, marketing, managerial and legal matters. In a nutshell, merchant banking provides a wide range of services for starting until running a business.

9) Write a detailed note on evolution and growth of merchant banking in India.

Ans: Formal merchant banking activity in India was originated in 1969 with the Merchant Banking Division set up by the Grindlays Bank, the then largest foreign bank in India. The main service by the merchant banks included the management of public issues and some aspects of financial consultancy. State Bank of India started merchant banking in 1973 followed by ICICI Lin 1974. The early and mid-seventies witnessed a boom in the growth of merchant banking organisation in the country with various commercial banks, financial institutions, brokers and firms entering into the field of merchant banking. The early growth of merchant banking in the country is assigned to the Foreign Exchange Regulation Act, 1973 (FERA) under which a large number of foreign companies in India were required to dilute their foreign holdings to continue business in the country. This had caused two-pronged effect, viz. firstly, in the form of spate in FERA issues eliciting interest of the investors by creating massive awareness about capital markets amongst the new class of investing public; secondly, merchant banking activity became attractive to banks and the firms of consultants and share brokers who entered into this field vigorously to reap the advantages of the expanding capital markets.

10) Mutual Funds: Mutual fund is fund (collection and saving of money resources) containing various Mutual Fund schemes introduced by the MF institution / trust who channelized the savings of large number of people to the corporate securities in such a way that the investor get steady return; capital appreciation; low risk; etc. (overall consideration of Mutual Fund and Mutual Fund Institution are same).

Mutual Fund Institution (UTI) -> create MF Units (schemes) -> for investors to invest. Schemes containing investment in different portfolio of securities. So MF institutions is a financial intermediary that serves as a link between investor and securities market.

Asset Management Company: A company that invests its client pooled funds into securities that match declared financial objectives (high return and low risk). It is the primary organ of the mutual fund company. It creates and manages new schemes considering low risk and high return, creating diversification of schemes.

What are the different types of mutual funds?

Ans. In accordance with the different objectives, mutual funds can be classified on the following basis:

Open - ended schemes: When the units are sold and repurchased continuously at net asset value (NAV) or NAV- related prices, then they are called open - ended schemes. These schemes are not required to be listed on stock exchange and hence, can offer repurchase just after allotment.

This scheme also offers the investors to enter and exit the scheme at any time during the life of the funds. Under open-ended schemes, there is no fixed corpus. The redemption period is also not fixed under open-ended schemes and hence, the scheme can be terminated, whenever it is required. This scheme even increases the liquidity of the investor, as the units under this scheme can be bought and sold continuously.

Close-ended schemes: The corpus under close - ended scheme is fixed having a stipulated maturity period of 2 to 5 years. Investors has the option of investing in the scheme at the time of its launching. A period not exceeding 45 days is fixed for the opening of such a scheme.

These are listed in the stock exchanges and thus from there, the units can be bought and sold. These schemes can, however, be converted into open-ended Schemes.

Interval scheme: This scheme constitutes the features of both the open-ended scheme and close-ended scheme. These schemes are open for sale or redemption during pre-determined intervals at NAV-related prices.

Income funds: Income funds aim to provide safety of investments and regular income to investors. It invests predominantly in income bearing securities such as debentures, commercial papers, government securities and bonds.

Growth funds: Growth funds are meant to appreciate capital over medium to long-term investors. It offers higher returns to investors in the long run and assumes risks associated with equity investments. However, it does not provide assurance or guarantee of returns.

Balanced funds: Balanced funds provide both regular income and capital appreciation. II balances the portfolio by dividing investments between equity shares and fixed interest-bearing instruments in an equitable proportion.

Money market mutual funds: Money market mutual funds provide high liquidity with low rate of return. It is specialised in making investment in short-term money market institutions, such as treasury bills and certificate of deposits.

Domestic funds: Domestic funds include those funds which mobilise resources from a particular geographical locality, especially a country. It has a limited scope and is confined to the boundaries of a nation.

Off - shore funds: Off-shore funds include those funds which attract foreign capital for investment in the country issuing company. It opens domestical capital market to facilitate cross-border fund flow from international investors.

What are the constituents of a mutual fund organisation?
Ans. The constituents of a mutual fund organisation are.
The Sponsor
The Trustees
The Asset Management Company
The Custodians

11) Depositories: A depository is an organization where the securities of a shareholder are kept in electronic data form as a traditional way of holding physical paper securities. By analogy a depository is a bank for securities like we keep money in bank here we keep securities in depository. Like SBI demat account, groww demat account, upstock etc.
The investor operates his account in a depository in much the same way as bank account. Investors who desires to participate in a depository have to open a duly introduced account with a depository participant. The account can be opened with 0 balance. The investor then hands over the securities for dematerialization. ie certificates are destroyed and equal number of securities are credited in the electronic holdings of the investor.
The participant is the representative of the investors in the depository system. It is like the stockbroker who trades on behalf of the client. Financial Institutions, banks, custodians become participants in the depository.
A depository is required to be a company under companies Act 2013 and depository participant must be registered under SEBI.

How many depositories are there in India? Discuss about the existing depositories in India.
Ans: At present, there are two depositories in India. They are:
(i) National Securities Depositories Limited (NSDL): NSDL was the first depository company set up in India. It was sponsored by the Unit Trust of India,

NSE, State Bank of India, HDFC Bank and Citi Bank. As it is a public limited company, the Board of Directors are entrusted with its management.

(ii) Central Depository Services Ltd. (CDSL): CDSL was promoted as the secondary depository in India for dealing in securities, in the electronic form, by the name of Central Depository Services (India) Limited (CDSL) by the Bombay Stock Exchange (BSE) in association with the Bank of India, Bank of Baroda, State Bank of India and HDFC Bank.

Mention the constituents of depository system.
Ans: The constituents of depository system are:
The Depository Participant
The Beneficial Owner/Investor
The Issuer
The Depository

Depository Receipt

1.Foreign Individual / Foreign company → invest →in certain country → that country's exchange depository →that country's currency → that country's shares → that receipt / acknowledgement of buying is called Depository Receipt (DR).

Donald Trump (FI) → Invest in India → India's exchange BSE → through an Indian depository (SBI) → shares (RIL) → it is called Indian Depository Receipt (IDR)

2. Indian Individual → invest → USA → NYSE (USA depository) →in dollars → shares of Apple → it is called American Depository Receipt (ADR)

3. Indian Individual → invest → UK → London Stock Exchange (UK depository) →in Euro → shares of HSBC → it is called Global Depository Receipt (GDR)

Who is a portfolio manager?
Ans: A portfolio manager is a body corporate who pursuant to a contract or arrangement with a client, advice undertakes on behalf of the client (whether as a discretionary portfolio manager or otherwise), the management or administration of a portfolio of securities or the funds of the client.

Bonds:

GDP linked bonds: Proposals during covid-19 pandemic for reviving the economy, these kinds of bonds were on talk of the market. These kinds of bonds will be issued by the government of India and will be linked to the country's GDP. The interest rate will be as per the country's gdp percentage with callable features and will be flexible in purchasing and selling of the bond. This callable feature generally means the government can repurchase the bond at any point of time.

Elephant bonds: A course of action/ path/ method for people of India to bring their money back, hoarded secretly in offshore without getting prosecuted. Once they declare their total offshore power, they will be asked to invest 40% of it on elephant bonds.
Execution: person A declared 1 cr of total offshore assets to the Government of India, then he has to invest 40% ie 40 lakhs in the elephant bonds. And on the remaining 60 cr, the govt will charge 15% tax i.e. 15 lakhs and the remaining 45 lakhs will be converted to white money. Now what about the return on these bonds, the Government will charge 75 % tax on the return of any amount invested on these bonds and the rest 25% will be the profit or dividend earned by the investor.
Those who declare their offshore hideout money will be immunized from foreign exchange, black money and taxation laws.

Electoral bonds: If a political party gets a donation of less than Rs 20000, than it wasn't mandatory for the party to reveal the source of fund as it was the sole rule existed before the 2017 annual budget which was further misused as accepted by various political parties. But after the roll out 2017 budget a massive change was introduced with electoral bonds.

If an entity/org/individual wants to donate funds to any political party which is above Rs 2000 than it should be in the form of electoral bonds rather than cash and the respective party have to reveal the source when asked.

Who can purchase the bonds: any person who is citizen of India; Incorporated or established in India. Person includes - Individual, HUF, Company, Firm, Association of persons, Body of individuals, Agency/firm of that person.

A person -> bank ->purchase bond -> donate to any party. (the bond amount will be deducted from his bank account)
(But it is in the person whether he wants his name to be on the bond or rather maintain his privacy as the details will be with bank already. And it is not mandatory for the political party to write the name of the person in their books too.)

Valuation: The bonds have respective face value and are available in the denominations of 1k 10k 1L 10L 1cr. The bonds will be valid for 15 days from the date of purchase and can be purchased in January, April, July and Oct of each year

The eligibility of political parties on receiving the donations as bonds are: Every party which is registered under sec 29A of the Representation of Peoples Act 1951 and has secured at least 1% of votes polled in the most recent ls or state election.
Supreme Court ruled out notice orders all political parties to disclose details of the donor of the bonds.

Blue bond: On Oct 29, 2018, The Republic of Syechelles introduced world's first sovereign blue bond, a financial instrument designed to support various sustainable marines and fisheries projects. The bond raised $15 million USD from the international market. The World Bank has helped the country in developing the bond and brought three initial investors - Calvert Impact Capital, Nuveen and Prudential Financial Inc.

Seychelles is an archipelagic island country in the Indian Ocean on the African continent and a part of African Union. The country consists of 115 islands. Its capital and largest city, Victoria.

AT-1 bonds (on the way for restructuring and revival of yes bank): AT-1 bonds are basically additional tier 1 bonds. When banks aren't able to meet the capital stated in Basel 3 norms, they raise additional tier 1 capital by issuing bonds. These are perpetual (never ending i.e. with no maturity date) bonds with a fixed higher annual coupon rate but are fully unsecured.
These bonds are listed and traded on exchanges. These are unsecured because the guidelines written in these bonds says about not paying any interest if the bank goes into further losses.

Perpetual consol or war bond:
Perpetual bond: This bond is a fixed income debt instrument with no fixed maturity date. It is issued by Government or entity for a lifetime basis or till the respective issuer declares maturity date. Since it lacks a fixed time period therefore it is more considered as equity rather than debt.
The major drawback in this bond is that it is not redeemable, that is the principal amount is not refundable till maturity and the major advantage is that a steady flow of interest keeps arriving forever.

In 1917 consol bonds were issued during world war 1 by the British treasury to raise funds for the war with an interest rate of 5% will now be finally redeemed after 100 years, the investors received interest for a century.

Government bonds are known as G- secs in India, Treasury in USA and Glits in UK.

Overseas sovereign bonds: Any form bond issue by the government is known as sovereign bond and the fixed interest received by the purchaser is known as yield. Like any other government bond this too has been issued by the same with a fixed rate of interest and for a particular time period.

This bond will be issued in the foriegn market denominated in foreign currency.

Nri bond: Basically these bonds are issued by Reserve Bank of India to the Non-Resident Indians to attract foreign investment and currencies in India. It is considered to be safest as issued by the Indian central bank.

Why does the government need to issue this? - as India is a huge importer of arms, crude oil, foreign goods, the country needs enough foreign currency to pay the balance of payments. Also, the funds received through NRI bonds will help the country in meeting Current account deficit.

Masala bonds: Masala bond is a rupee denominated bond. When an Indian company issues rupee denominated bond in the overseas market.

As the purchaser will be an overseas individual so the risk too falls on him because of the fluctuations of the currency exchange rate.

Helps in deepening the Indian financial system, internationalization of rupee, stability of rupee. The first masala bonds was issued by International Finance Corporation in 2013

Green bonds: Climate change is real and by far the biggest challenge presently the world is facing. The required sustainability to control the CO_2 emission and maintain proper environmental protection required huge amount of funds by each of the respective Governments around the world. So to make funds little easier a new financial product is introduced by the name Green bonds. These bonds are similar to regular bonds but these are issued to finance green projects or activities. Any company which works on green and clean environment projects can issue green bonds. for eg: solar energy wind energy hydro energy climate adaptation process etc. The market for green bonds has rose to 30.5 billion dollars as of 2014 and most of make it to Europe.

Rhino Impact Bonds: These bonds are introduced for the conservation of endangered bicornis rhino or the black rhino by the London Zoological Society which aims to increase the population and the investors will be only rewarded if the number of these animals rise. The 50-million-dollar RIB is the world's first financial instrument working on conservation. This $50 million will be divided into bonds of several small values which the investors can opt for purchase. These rhinos are native to eastern and southern Africa including Zimbabwe, Malawi, Botswana, South Africa, Kenya, Mozambique, Tanzania and Namibia. This animal is Critically Endangered on the IUCN list and just left to 5500 presently from 65000 in 1970. These rhinos are killed for their horns which is sold in the black market for huge values. The amount collected on selling these bonds will be used for building five new secretive spaces or wildlife sanctuaries for the rhinos.

It is believed that huge corporations will come forward and invest in conservation of wildlife through their CSR funds as big giants are only after profit so if they earn it through conservation then it will be a win-win situation for both the corporations and the sustainability of the environment.

Some Questions:

1. Section __________ of the Banking Regulations Act, 1949 defines banking companies.
Ans: 5

2. Which of the following is not a characteristic of financial services?
Ans: stability of demand

3. Which of the following bodies set up the Regional Rural Banks (RRBs) in India?
Ans: state govt

4. When was Industrial Reconstruction Bank of India (IRBI) established?
Ans: 1985

5. In which state was the first state Industrial Development Corporations (SIDC) established.
Ans: Andhra Pradesh

6. Name an investment company in India.
Ans: UTI

7. In which year was SFC established?
Ans: 1951

8. What is the full form of FACS in SBI FACS Ltd.?
Ans: factors and commercial services

9. Which of the following institutions is not a credit rating agency?
Ans: SICOM

10. Which of the following is an organised non-banking financial institution?
Ans: All India Development Financial Institution

11. Which of the following is not true about IFCI?
Ans: promotion of public ownership

12. IDBI is a wholly owned subsidiary
Ans: RBI (Reserve Bank of India)

13. Which of the following is true about operating lease?
Ans: cancellable

14. Who among the following is not a party to foreign lease?
Ans: broker

15. Which of the following is a disadvantage of leasing?
Ans: cost

16. A project should be accepted, if its NPV is
Ans: greater than 1

17. Accounting Standard (AS) _____ prescribes for lessees and lessors.

Ans: 19

18. Which of the following is not a feature of hire purchase?
Ans: hire charges are fluctuating

19. Which of the following is an element of leasing?
Ans: Number of Parties

20. Primary lease is also known as _________ lease.
Ans: front-ended

21. The internal rate of return is the rate of discount at which the present value of cash inflows is _____ to the present value of cash outflows.
Ans: equal

22. Which of the following is a sale and leaseback leasing?
Ans: sale of an asset already owned by a firm.

23. An operating lease is a lease other than a _________ lease.
Ans: financial

24. SUA stands for
Ans: Stockbroker Underwriter's Association

25. When was CRISIL set up?
Ans: 1987

26. Category IV Merchant Bankers can act as
Ans: consultant

27. In which year was merchant banking started in India?
Ans: 1967

28. Discount and Finance House of India was formed under the __________.
Ans: Companies Act, 1956

29. Capital adequacy norms is applicable to applicants whose net worth is more than _____ financial results.
Ans: 5

30. Every merchant banker shall furnish to the Board _______ financial results.
Ans: half yearly

31. Which of the following is not a pre-issue activity involved in issue management?
Ans: stock investment

32. What is the fee payable for application for registration of merchant banker
Ans: Rs 25,000/-?

33. Who appoints the compliance officer?
Ans: merchant banker

34. Not a role of a merchant banker.
Ans: broker

35. In which country did merchant banking evolved?
Ans: Europe

36. Open-ended schemes/funds provides better _______ to the investors.
Ans: Liquidity

37. Which of the following is not an advantage of mutual funds?
Ans: rigidity

38. In which year was mutual fund started in India?
Ans: 1964

39. Name a scheme of LIC Mutual Fund.
Ans: Dhanvridhi

40. When was SBI Mutual Fund launched?
Ans: 1987

41. Which of the following is not a constituent of mutual fund?
Ans: underwriter

42. The sponsor must contribute at least _____ % of the net worth of AMC (Asset Management Company)
Ans: 40

43. Expense ratio in the mutual funds can be calculated as
Ans: Total expenses / Average net assets

44. What is the application fee for registration of a mutual fund by a sponsor?
Ans: Rs 1 lakh

45. Who performs the task of designing and marketing of mutual fund by a sponsor?
Ans: Asset Management Company

46. Which of the following is a type of mutual fund according to the scheme of operation.
Ans: Open - ended scheme

47. _________ started mutual fund in India.
Ans: Unit Trust of India (UTI).

48. Which of the following is not a mode of finance by venture capitalists?
Ans: debentures.

49. Which of the following is a part of early-stage financing of venture capital?
Ans: second round financing.

50. In case of physical shares, stamp duty of _______ % is payable on transfer.
Ans: 0.5

51. In venture capital, investment is _______.
Ans: illiquid

52. Which institution set up the Risk Capital Foundation (RCE) in India?

Ans: IFCI

53. A depository participant is a _____ of a depository.
Ans: Agent

54. What is the annual fee required to be paid by the depository annually?
Ans: Rs 10 lakh

55. NEST stands for
Ans: National Electronic Settlement and Transfer

56. From which year has SEBI made compulsory trading of shares of listed companies in stock exchanges in demat form?
Ans: 2002

57. Name a money market instrument.
Ans: commercial bills

58. Name a depository participant.
Ans: Bank

THANK YOU
KEEP SUPPORTING
Follow Us
YOUTUBE
FACEBOOK
INSTAGRAM